Praise for *Magick for All Seasons*

"There have been several Wheel of the Year guidebooks in the last several years—each one different than the last, each one bringing us into a deeper connection to the world around and within us. Marla Brook's *Magick for All Seasons* allows us to glimpse a world both glorious and simple—one that takes us by the hand and walks with the reader through the beauty of these natural and ancient celebrations. I especially loved the dedication to her great-grandma Sophie. A terrific addition to your personal library."

—H. Byron Ballard, author of *Seasons of a Magical Life* and *A Feral Church*

"Marla Brooks has crafted a down-to-earth collection of Witch Wisdom, blending history, practical spellwork, and personal anecdotes, all hung skillfully upon the Wheel of the Year. The inclusion of Great-Grandma Sophie's witchy tips adds a charming touch, making the reader feel as though they are receiving teachings from a trusted elder. This is the kind of book I devoured growing up. It is sure to add spice to anyone's practice."

—Jason Miller, author of *Consorting with Spirits* and other works

"A sweet ode to the author's great grandmother, *Magick for All Seasons* offers a trove of spells and recipes for those who are curious about celebrating Pagan seasonal holidays. Marla Brooks has created a delightfully homey grimoire filled to the brim with a ready-made collection of ideas to make each season a little more magical."

—Christine Grace, author of *The Witch at the Forest's Edge*

"*Magick for All Seasons* is a personal, pragmatic guide to filling your year with magic. From seasonal lore to magical correspondences, each chapter introduces the themes and symbols of the Wheel of the Year. This book is packed with hands-on activities; you'll find spells, rituals, divination, recipes, and so much more. I look forward to returning to this book again and again for inspiration in my own seasonal magick."

—Nicholas Pearson, author of *The Witching Stones*

"A consistent voice of wisdom and support for the Pagan path, Marla Brooks has offered us another gift. *Magick for All Seasons* is a new take on classic concepts and will be invaluable to witches now and in the future."

—Courtney Weber, author of *Hekate: Goddess of Witches*

Magick for All Seasons

A Grimoire for the Wheel of the Year

MARLA BROOKS

Foreword by Lorriane Anderson

WEISER BOOKS

This edition first published in 2025 by Weiser Books, an imprint of
Red Wheel/Weiser, LLC
With offices at:
65 Parker Street, Suite 7
Newburyport, MA 01950
www.redwheelweiser.com

Copyright © 2025 by Marla Brooks
Foreword by Lorriane Anderson, copyright © 2025 by Red Wheel/Weiser
All rights reserved. No part of this publication may be reproduced or transmitted in any form or by any means, electronic or mechanical, including photocopying, recording, or by any information storage and retrieval system, nor used in any manner for purposes of training artificial intelligence (AI) technologies to generate text or imagery, including technologies that are capable of generating works in the same style or genre, without permission in writing from Red Wheel/Weiser, LLC. Reviewers may quote brief passages.

ISBN: 978-1-57863-850-5
Library of Congress Cataloging-in-Publication Data available upon request.

Cover design by Sky Peck Design
Interior photos by Marla Brooks
Interior by Debby Dutton
Typeset in Jensen Pro and Mr Eaves San
Printed in the United States of America
IBI
10 9 8 7 6 5 4 3 2 1

This book contains advice and information for using herbs in spells and folk remedies and is not meant to diagnose, treat, or prescribe. It should be used to supplement, not replace, the advice of your physician or other trained healthcare practitioner. If you know or suspect you have a medical condition, are experiencing physical symptoms, or if you feel unwell, seek your physician's advice before embarking on any medical program or treatment. Readers are cautioned to follow instructions carefully and accurately for the best effect. Readers using the information in this book do so entirely at their own risk, and the author and publisher accept no liability if adverse effects are caused.

DEDICATION

Be Forewarned

Within these pages, you'll find references to Great-Grandma Sophie. She isn't a made-up character. She was a living, breathing wise woman, a.k.a. witch. She was my great grandmother. Great-Grandma Sophie will be popping in occasionally with words of wisdom and advice. You may also find that you feel her presence in other ways.

Sophie was born in 1853 in West Prussia and was said to be the wise woman of her village. When I was little, my grandfather never spoke of his mother in front of me. It was only behind closed doors and away from my young ears, but young ears often sneak into grownups' conversations, and that's when I heard the story that Grandpa's mother was a witch. I was overjoyed to know there was a witch in the family.

As stories about her were rare, I didn't know much more about her, but my mother eventually told me that before Sophie passed away in 1934, she wanted to pass her knowledge down to her daughter, my great-aunt Manya, who wanted nothing to do with it, and so Sophie took her wisdom to the grave.

In our custom, newborns are named after deceased relatives and I was named after Manya—Marla is the English translation of the name. Was it coincidence that a few generations skipped, and I picked up where Sophie left off? Maybe.

This grimoire is written for Sophie. She couldn't share her wisdom, but I hope this book will suffice.

Oh, one more thing. Don't be surprised if you feel someone looking over your shoulder while you're using this book. It's only Sophie wanting to say hello.

CONTENTS

Foreword by Lorriane Anderson	ix
Acknowledgments	xiii
Introduction	xv
The Wheel of the Year	xix
Part I　　Samhain—October 31	1
Part II　　Yule—December 19–24	39
Part III　　Imbolc—February 1st	67
Part IV　　Ostara—March 19–22	87
Part V　　Beltane—May 1	111
Part VI　　Litha—June 19–22	131
Part VII　　Lughnasadh/Lammas—August 1	157
Part VIII　Mabon—September 19–22	177

Appendix

A Glossary of Witchcraft Terminology, Crystals, and Candles	209
Recommended Reading	223
Guide to Practices, Spells, and Recipes	225

FOREWORD

The seasons are very dear to me. I have always observed the changing of the seasons intently, perhaps because we don't experience seasons in Los Angeles, where myself and Marla live, the way many others do. There will be no snow unless you'd like to drive two hours up the side of a very big mountain; no, thank you, heights are not my friend. And the trees don't really change their color so much as they're green one day and gone the next. But you can see traditional signs of each season here if you're keen to pay attention and know where to look.

My attempts to connect with the seasons more organically led me to the Wheel of the Year. It was the first time I can honestly remember seeing the obvious connection between my life and that of the earth's. I came to better understand the process and even beauty of death by observing plants in their nakedness, following Samhain. I learned to look for signs of hope by listening to the birds chirping outside of my window in the small hours of the morning about the same time as Imbolc. I knew if they were singing, spring wasn't far behind.

Eventually, the seasons taught me how to honor the changing of my personal cycles in life. That they were almost identical to the shifting of the earth's seasons. And then, I learned how to utilize the seasons to aid me or support me in my endeavors. That you can harness the energy of the seasons and that there are wise ones who have been doing this for ages. It was an epiphany that changed the course of my life. Now, it's not just something I do in my spare time but my career, my practice, and my lifestyle. I see the seasons in everything I do.

I was knee-deep into winter when I first started reading this book. The season had been unusually cold and rainy in Los Angeles, one of the most winter-like seasons we've had in a very long time. Yet I found myself spiritually in a spring cycle. I was in a period of growth, renewal, and forward movement. It was what I believe to be the best winter season of my life even though winter is traditionally very challenging for me. In contrast, the winter prior was probably the worst winter season I've ever had.

About halfway through this book, which happened to be just a little more than halfway through winter, the true magick of *Magick for All Seasons* became apparent to me. I'm convinced it was Great-Grandma Sophie who fostered my aha moment! You'll meet her in these pages shortly. This is a rather delicious collection of spells, information, recipes, incantations, and rituals to support you in your journey, regardless of what season you find yourself in. A grimoire that offers the perfect spell or practice for any and all days of the year.

The Wheel of the Year is the witch's way of observing and honoring the shift of the seasons. Each of the eight sacred days, or what you might know as sabbats, represents a critical point on the journey that each year ushers us through. But like all things on earth, the changing of the seasons holds a mirror to the human experience. It goes beyond knowing when it will snow or when days will warm or when to harvest your garden.

The Wheel of the Year is Mother Nature gently taking your hand, sometimes wrapping you in her warm embrace, and sometimes giving you a right proper shove, letting you know no season, good or bad, will last forever.

Spring will follow winter as surely as night will turn into day. Each season offers its fair share of challenges but also glorious magick. The biggest takeaway from the Wheel of the Year is that your life will ebb and flow just as plants drop their seeds, grow, lose their leaves, die in winter, and grow back again. Your life experiences all of the seasons in the human way. There will be times when you're expanding your orbit and it feels like it will go on forever—like the sun has taken permanent residence in your spirit. There will be other times when you are in a winter-like season, experiencing a dark night of hardship or frustration, or perhaps just a deep need to rest.

Sometimes your personal season will match that on the calendar but often times it won't. The Wheel of the Year marks specific times of the year, that's true, but I believe its true magick isn't to describe when to experience a season, it simply helps you to understand what season you're in and how best to navigate it.

And when you know what season your soul is experiencing, grab this book. It has everything you could possibly need to navigate anything you're going through. Should you need protection, more money, a birthday spell, to unclutter your mind, or even help packing for a trip, Marla—and her Great-Grandma Sophie, of course—have you covered.

If you want to learn more about witchcraft, divination, or why you should never step into a faerie ring (I didn't know this was a thing and am hoping I haven't done it, eek!), you will find all of this and more within these pages. And of course, if you need inspiration to honor the actual shifting of the seasons as the calendar sees them, you'll find that here too! There are plenty of sabbat-specific goodies to support you as you work your magick through the turning of the year.

Magick for All Seasons is your trusted companion. It is destined to live on my altar for years to come and I recommend the same to anyone looking to work with the seasons for growth, healing, happiness, and navigating the complexities of life. Whether you're just getting started with learning to live in a magickal way or you're looking for a rich resource of witchy ideas, this book has something to get you through any and all seasons of life. It is my absolute pleasure to introduce this book to you. Blessed Be, my darling.

—Lorriane Anderson, author and teacher of the spiritual arts

ACKNOWLEDGMENTS

I'm very lucky. There are a group of people in my life who nourish my mind and soul in so many ways. We're all like-minded, but don't always agree on everything, and that's a blessing in disguise. By respecting each other's differences and keeping an open mind, we learn, and learning is a gift. As there are way too many to list here, I'm going to mention those who helped me in putting this grimoire together: Judika Illes, Tim Shaw, Barbara Duncan, and Sam Miller.

My mentors Stanley Ralph Ross and Kenny Kingston need to be acknowledged as well. Stanley taught me all about the writing life, and Kenny taught me about the afterlife. They are both on the Other Side now, but I know they're still around.

And finally, thanks and appreciation go to all the guests who have joined me each week on my podcast, *Stirring the Cauldron*, since 2008, sharing your wisdom from every aspect of the metaphysical world. You've taught me so much.

INTRODUCTION

There's one thing everyone needs in their lives: a little magick. Turn the pages of this bewitched and enchanted grimoire to explore the seasons of the witch with each turn of the Wheel of the Year by way of magickal spells and practices.

I'm calling this book a grimoire, but what is the difference between a grimoire and a Book of Shadows? Many have asked this question, and now I will answer it. Let's look at the similarities and the differences between the two.

Gerald Gardner, the "father of Wicca," allegedly first introduced the Book of Shadows to people whom he had initiated into the Craft through his Bricket Wood coven in the 1940s and 50s. (It would later become a pop culture term due in part to hit TV shows like *Charmed*.) He claimed that it was a personal cookbook of spells that worked for him, and he passed them down to coven members. Others, however, beg to differ. Some people claim that Books of Shadows are generally handed down from generation to generation in their families, hundreds and hundreds of years back, with each generation adding to it. So how could Books of Shadows have been passed down for hundreds of years if Gerald Gardner first introduced the book some eighty years ago?

Grimoires go back quite a bit farther. The term "grimoire" originates from the French word *Grammaire*. It means a book that's written in Latin. It wasn't until the 18th century that *grimoire* began to be used to refer to historical books of magick. The earliest known magickal text we're currently aware of dates back to ancient Mesopotamia, where incantations were inscribed on cuneiform clay tablets. The practice of writing about magick continued to ancient Egypt and later to Greece and Rome, but magickal texts were not yet written in book form until the medieval period and were said to be created by figures such as ceremonial magician Dr. John Dee, who was a teacher, mathematician, astronomer, astrologer, occultist, and alchemist. He was also the scientific and medical adviser to Queen Elizabeth I.

To simplify things, perhaps we can distinguish the two books by saying that the major difference is the personal connection. A grimoire is a textbook of general knowledge for all to read. A Book of Shadows is literally that: a shadow of its owner, detailing their personal path, beliefs, spells, and rituals, not to be shared with anyone without consent.

I consider this book to be a mash-up grimoire. The pages of this book are filled with general knowledge, spells, incantations, exercises, recipes, and all sorts of goodies—all circling the Wheel of the Year—so call it what you may.

Blessed Be!

A Bit of Grimoire Trivia

Close your eyes and picture in your mind's eye your perfect image of a grimoire. You are walking down a winding path to find it—perhaps a forgotten corridor in an ancient library, or maybe the windy, wooded pathway to a witch's secluded cabin. Either way, you wind up trailing your fingers along a shelf filled with books until—there it is. What does it look like? Perhaps you envision a dusty leather-bound book, covered in cobwebs. Perhaps it is ornately decorated, with an intricate symbol made out of gemstones in the center. Perhaps it is bound in thick chains, as if warning you—reader, beware, magick be here.

But is that really what a grimoire is? Some legends claim that grimoires must be in the form of a manuscript, written in red ink (or possibly in blood), or they must be bound in black leather—or in human skin. Obviously, this is all very fanciful, but it does make for good storytelling as any number of fantasy novels or Hollywood productions can tell you.

Where did grimoires actually originate? Some historians believe that the origin of the grimoire was the Greek Magical Papyri, also known as the PGM. The Greek Magical Papyri, so named by scholars, is a collection of papyri from Graeco-Roman Egypt, written between 100 and 400 CE. The PGM contains magickal spells, rituals, hymns, and formulas. Heinrich Cornelius Agrippa, the famous German Renaissance polymath, physician, and philosopher, was a great student of the occult and wrote his own grimoire, *Three Books of Occult Philosophy*, in 1533.

Possibly the most famous of all grimoires is *The Key of Solomon*, a pseudepigraphical grimoire said to be written by King Solomon himself. It contains a series of pentacles for performing magickal operations. The most well-known translation is by Samuel Liddell "MacGregor" Mathers, a British occultist and the founder of the Golden Dawn. (Though most likely, it was Mathers's wife, Moina Mathers nee Bergson, who provided—or at the very least, greatly assisted—the translation for the Hebrew in *The Key of Solomon*. Moina Mathers came from a prominent Jewish family and was well-versed in the Hebrew language.)

The Grand Grimoire, also known as *La Dragon Rouge* (*The Red Dragon*) or *The Great Grimoire*, is a medieval grimoire that truly does have a grand reputation, as it is believed to be one of the most powerful and fearsome magickal books of all time. *The Grand Grimoire* is divided into two books. The first contains instructions for summoning a demon— Lucifer, to be exact—and subduing the demon so that the demon might do the user's bidding. The second book is also divided into two more parts; the first describes the process by which to make a pact with the demon, and the second contains spells, rituals, and magickal potions to be done after completing the first book. *The Grand Grimoire* makes mention of three greater demons—Lucifer, Beelzebub, and Astaroth—and six lesser demons—Lucifuge Rofocale, Satanachia, Agaliarept, Fleurèty, Sargatanas, and Nebiros. Spells included inside involve any number of lofty goals from winning the lottery to making oneself invisible to winning the heart of a fair maiden. This grimoire was featured on the TV series *Sleepy Hollow*, where it was once owned by a fictionalized version of John Dee.

The Sworn Book of Honorius is a medieval grimoire that's said to be written by a magician named Honorius of Thebes. It too contains lengthy operations for summoning demons and a number of spells for all kinds of purposes. While *Sleepy Hollow* portrayed John Dee as having owned *The Grand Grimoire*, he actually did once own the oldest preserved copy of the *The Sworn Book of Honorius*.

And now, you have this grimoire that I have personally prepared for you: a grimoire dedicated to the Wheel of the Year.

THE WHEEL OF THE YEAR

The Wheel of the Year is a term that is used to refer to the changing of the seasons. Each season is marked by a series of holy days called sabbats to honor the qualities of each time of the year, life's lessons as revealed through nature, and our relationship with the god and goddess. These holy days are divided into what is termed the Greater Sabbats and the Lesser Sabbats, which reflect the themes of birth, death, and rebirth. The spokes of the Wheel are comprised of the four Greater and four Lesser Sabbats. There are eight sabbats in total. The cycle completes and then begins again.

The Greater Sabbats, which begin at sundown of the previous day, are Samhain, Imbolc, Beltane, and Lughnasadh/Lammas. The Greater Sabbats are highly spiritual occasions, undertaken with the greatest regard and dignity. The Wheel of the Year is seen to begin at Samhain, the Celtic New Year, which is also known as Halloween or All Hallows Eve.

The Lesser Sabbats are the equinoxes and the solstices. They consist of Yule (the Winter Solstice), Ostara (the Spring/Vernal Equinox), Litha (the Summer Solstice), and Mabon (the Fall/Autumnal Equinox). These sabbats, although called lesser, should not to be thought of as any less spiritually important or significant than the Greater Sabbats. These are the points when the lessons of balance and their specific place in time take on a greater meaning.

PART I

Samhain—October 31

Samhain, or Halloween, is the final harvest of the year. To witches and Pagans, it is our most holy and sacred sabbat and is considered our New Year. The commencing of the season of darkness, it is the festival of death, and as such, it is the celebration of the eternal cycle, for without death there can be no rebirth. This is the time that the new cycle truly begins and the Wheel begins to turn again from the start. Samhain is the time of introspection; it is the time to assess and retune us to the belief in the oneness of all spirits and in our firm resolution that physical death is not the final act of existence. The veil between the worlds—the consciousness which separates the land of the living from the land of the dead—is at its thinnest. We remember and honor our loved ones and ancestors; we release the spirits of those we have lost. We mourn, but at the same time we rejoice because this is the triumph of life!

Celtic countries originally celebrated this feast of the dead. They would leave food as offerings on altars or doorsteps for the wandering dead, for whom the veil was thin. Candles were left burning in windows to guide the spirits, ancestors, and loved ones. Many practitioners today have carried on these practices, using this sacred time to honor their dead.

Samhain is a cross-quarter day—a day that falls directly between the solstice and the equinox—a time outside of time, the night that is not a night, but instead a powerful time of fluctuation and change. It's a good night for candle magick, astral projection, past-life work, and dark-moon mysteries. Sit in contemplation with the night and the coming winter.

Samhain is a powerful night for divination. It's a great night for you to indulge in your favorite way to divine: casting runes, I Ching, scrying, using a pendulum, automatic writing, a tarot or other card reading. It's also a wonderful time to practice your favorite way to speak with those on the other side.

Symbols: Jack-o'-lanterns, black cats, ghosts and ancestral spirits, the waning moon, the dark mysteries, and rebirth through death

Activities: Build a bonfire, practice all forms of divination, and visit the graves of your loved ones

Incense: Myrrh, patchouli, copal, sandalwood, sweetgrass, and wormwood

Spell Work: Spells to keep anything negative from the past—evil, harm, corruption, greed—out of the future. A good time to cast mirror spells of reflection, protection spells, spells for uncrossing and clearing obstacles, manifesting, transformation, and creative visualization.

Deities: Hecate, Persephone, Lilith, Hel, Loki, and Anubis

Gemstones: Black onyx, smoky quartz, bloodstone, carnelian, and obsidian

Trees, Fruits, and Herbs: Allspice, nutmeg, apples, pumpkins, turnips, gourds, mistletoe, and willow trees

Animals: Bat, black cat, owl, wolves, and raven

Colors: Black, orange, gold, and purple

Great-Grandma Sophie's Witchy Tips

Witches' homes are living beings. Every household isn't full of just humans—spirits and deities are also sharing this space. Often, they are most active around Samhain. These spirits and deities are there to care for and protect us, so we should not ignore them. Whenever you enter your home, say "hello" out loud, and when you leave, say, "Thank you for watching over the house when I'm gone." If you ignore the good entities in your house, you're leaving it wide open for negative energies and spirits to hang around. The following are ways you can repel malicious beings and invite or help friendly ones.

- Hang witch hazel in doorways and windows for protection and to keep out malevolent influences and negative energies. This works for any heavy emotions you are feeling in your life, as the magickal properties of witch hazel will help you to find emotional balance.
- Regular cleaning and shifting of your supplies and tools allow the energy to continue to flow. Leaving things untouched for long periods of time stops the magickal flow through these items, and their energy becomes stagnant.
- Light a candle with your right hand to bring good luck and with your left hand to banish unwanted energy.
- Being outside on a rainy or windy day is a great way to cleanse yourself. Visualize the rain or wind passing through you, carrying away any negative energy that might be clinging to you.
- Lockets can be wearable protection charms depending on what's inside. Fill them with herbs, sigils, or incantations.
- Keep an ivy plant in your house. This plant grows in weblike patterns that will catch negative energy in your home. It doesn't matter

what type of ivy, but just remember to prune it regularly to get rid of negative buildup.

- Wash your front door with warm water and essential oils of rosemary and spearmint to invite good vibes, love, wisdom, and protection into your home.

- On the first of every month, write your goals and intentions on a bay leaf and then burn it. Throw the ashes out of your front door and ask the universe to bring these things to you.

- Place scissors under your bed, opened in the form of a cross or X, to cut and destroy any spiritual attack made against you while you are sleeping.

- If you don't have a fireplace, your stove is your hearth. Burning six white candles on your stove honors the heart of the home and appeases your house spirits. It is also a great tribute to the past hearth witches.

- String hawthorn berries on a black string and hang them above windows and doors to prevent spirits from entering your home in the astral state.

- Banish ghosts, evil spirits, or bad energy by placing a clove of garlic in each of a room's four corners. As the garlic absorbs the negativity it will begin to wither. At that point, take it outside and bury it.

Building an Ancestor Altar

The ancestors are venerated in many cultures and traditions. For Pagans, Samhain is the best time to build an altar for the ancestors, although of course you can build an altar at any time that feels "right" to you. Samhain is a preferable time because this sabbat and the days leading up to it are when the veil between our world and the spirit world is at its most thin and fragile. Setting up an ancestor shrine is a way to honor your ancestors—whether they be blood related or not. There are many kinds of ancestors; if you choose, you can erect an altar for spiritual teachers, mentors, beloved friends, or those you feel to be your spiritual kin. Your ancestors deserve respect and remembrance and this is a powerful and meaningful way to honor them. The altar may be used seasonally or as a permanent place in your home.

You will need:

- Photos and/or belongings of your ancestors

- A place where your altar can be left undisturbed so that the spirits of your ancestors may gather there and you can take time to meditate and honor them without having to move things around every time someone needs to use the table

- Incense for cleansing

The altar should be put together to your liking. Get as creative as you like. Some believe that salt or a picture of a living person should not be on your ancestor altar. It's believed that spirits will not come around where there is salt and that you should never place the living among the dead. You can do some research into various traditions and decide what's right for you. It's your altar and all up to you.

Choose photos that have meaning. Try to arrange the photos so that you can see all of them at once. Any objects belonging to one's deceased ancestors are completely appropriate with or without the photos.

The simple way to cleanse and consecrate the altar and make it a sacred space is to use a sage herb bundle, frankincense, or sandalwood incense. Some people prefer myrrh because myrrh smoke brings the astral realms closer to earth, opening a spiritual doorway. As the herb bundle or incense burns, offer up a prayer to the ancestors in your own words or use the following:

"Ancestor spirits, I call to you and welcome you. Your blood runs in my veins, your spirit is in my heart, your memories are in my soul. With this altar of remembrance, you'll never be forgotten. You live on within me and within those who are yet to come."

Samhain—October 31

Spend a little bit of time each day at the altar. Sit, meditate, and reflect. Be patient and see who might come through or what messages they send to you.

Spirit Guides

Spirit guides are benevolent beings that exist in the spiritual realm and offer guidance and support to individuals on their life path. Creating a relationship with our guides and learning how to communicate with them allow us to access their wisdom and guidance.

I was taught that when we are born, we have one spirit guide that stays with us throughout our lives, and others come in and out as needed. In layman's terms, it's like when we go to see our primary care doctor, a general practitioner, who evaluates our conditions and takes care of the mundane kind of ailments. When a special need comes up, our PC will refer us to a specialist. That's the same as with our spirit guides, except that we don't have to go through any necessary paperwork and wait weeks in advance to make the appointment.

Spirit guides come in varied shapes and sizes. There are major guides and minor guides. The difference between them is that major guides typically accompany us throughout our lives and help us to learn major life lessons. Minor guides are temporary and help with daily concerns or issues that we struggle with. It's debatable as to how many types of guides there are, but some of the majors include archangels, guardian angels, animal spirits, ascended masters, departed loved ones, and helper angels.

Some others that you can ask for are:

- **Protector Guide:** helps when you need courage and strength

- **Message Bearer:** assists you when you need to find information or to develop your psychic skills

- **Gatekeeper Guide:** provides physical and psychic protection when you're communicating with the spirit world

- **Teacher Guide:** helps you learn the life lessons you need for spiritual growth

- **Joy Guide:** helps you lighten up when you're going through a difficult time

- **Healing or Doctor Guide:** helps you improve your emotional, physical, and spiritual health

Some add extraterrestrials to that list as well.

Some of the most prominent spirit guides are ancestor guides. While you may not know of many of those who came before you, your ancestors in spirit know about you. They are full of wisdom and care about your progress and can help with healing and inherited karma. Call on them when you require extra strength or clarity.

For whatever reason, people may go through a lifetime and never try to touch base with their guides, but even so, they are always there, and you can call upon them at any time. If you've never tried to contact your guide, the first step is having an open mind, believing they are around, and acknowledging their presence. So how do you make contact and know when you've connected?

Look and listen for signs. There will be signs and symbols that have personal meaning to you. You can also ask them for a particular sign. Once the connection with a guide is made, you'll be able to feel the signs. Many people just feel their presence in different ways. I have a friend that gets goosebumps on her left arm when their guard is around. I always get the feeling that someone is right behind me.

I used to meditate a lot in past years and, at one point, slacked off for a few weeks. One of my teachers asked me if I was keeping up with my meditation. I mumbled that I wasn't and got a stern lecture.

That night, around midnight, I went into my home office, turned off all the lights, and lit a white candle and some incense. Living alone at the time, the serene environment, especially at midnight, was very comforting. I cleared my mind and after about two minutes or so, I suddenly felt somebody's hand gently squeezing my shoulder. It was the kind of squeeze you get when your parents want to show that you've done something very good.

That feeling of being touched broke my concentration, and when I turned around, nobody was there. To my surprise, I wasn't scared. I felt

Samhain—October 31

safe and, after giving it some thought, I chalked up the happening to one of my guides showing their pleasure that I took my teacher's advice. It was their way of reminding me that they are always watching over us.

Divination

"Every real discovery made, every serious and significant decision ever reached, was reached and made by divination."
—D. H. LAWRENCE

"Divination is not seeing the future; it's looking at the present from a different perspective and seeing connections that were otherwise invisible."
—CHARBEL TADROS

Samhain is the best time to practice divination, and there are many, many ways to practice it. Divination is the attempt to gain insight into a question or situation by way of an occultic, standardized process or ritual and has been used in various forms throughout history. Diviners gather their interpretations of how a querent should proceed by reading signs, symbols, events, and omens, or through supposed contact with the supernatural.

Automatic Writing
Automatic writing is a practice in which a person enters a state of altered consciousness, or a trance state, in order to produce writing that is prophetic or spiritual in nature, essentially letting a spirit guide their hand.

My Grandma Grace, on the other side of my family, had an ongoing automatic writing conversation with the same spirit for twenty years. I have pages and pages of the original writing and transcriptions that one of her other granddaughters copied to make the messages easier to read.

These days, it's not unusual for people to use their computers to do their automatic writing sessions. I was a bit dubious when I heard about that, so I tried myself to see if it's possible and it is!

All you need to do is find a quiet spot, open up your Microsoft Word or any other word processor that you use, put your hands lightly on the keyboard, close your eyes, and relax. It might take a session or two for any results, but there will come a time that your fingers will do the walking over the keyboard.

Ceromancy
Ceromancy is the practice of divination by candle wax. You will need one candle in the color that fits your question (like green for money, red for love, etc.) and a sheet of white paper. If you're using a white candle, however, choose a dark-colored paper instead. Light the candle and hold it upright over the paper. While the wax is melting at the tip, ask your question three times and then quickly tilt the candle so that the melted wax will spill on the paper. The pattern formed by the wax can be then interpreted as you see it.

Egg Divination
Egg divination uses the white of an egg. Take an egg and prick it on the top and bottom with a needle or pin. Allow three drops of the egg white to drip into a full glass of water. Over the next few hours, the white will spread through the glass, forming shapes, letters, or numbers, which can be then interpretated.

Oil Divination
Oil divination is the practice of divining using oil. Various forms of oil are used, but olive oil is the most common. In oil divination, you sit down at the table with a bowl of water in front of you, then slowly pour a bit of oil into the water. A teaspoon or so is plenty. The oil will rise and float on the water's surface. Watch it for a few moments. There are many different ways to interpret the shapes.

- If the oil divides into two sections, an argument may be in the offing.

- If the oil forms a ring and remains unbroken, a business journey will be profitable, or the sick will recover. This can also be taken as a positive response to a question.

- If small droplets of water emerge from the large one, it may indicate pregnancy. This is also a favorable sign for the sick, as it predicts recovery.

- If the oil spreads thinly and covers the entire surface of the water, beware of troubles ahead.

- Many small kinds of unconnected globules of oil indicate the coming of money.

- A crescent or star shape is extremely fortunate.

Burnings Divination

Write a question concerning the future on a small piece of paper. Place it face down on a flat, fireproof surface. Light one corner of the paper with a match. If the entire paper burns, the answer is yes. If only part of the paper burns, the answer is no.

Divination by Leaves

Write a question on a leaf and place it in a safe spot. If it quickly withers and dries, the prospects aren't good. If the leaf stays fresh and dries slowly, then the prospects are good.

Astrology

Samhain is a good time to look to the stars and contemplate what they say. Most witches already practice some sort of cosmic witchcraft because many follow moon cycles and often use astrological energies to enhance spellcasting. As we say, "As above, so below." That is commonly understood to mean that celestial movements and energies affect terrestrial events.

Some witches harness the power of the zodiac signs in their spell work by carving the symbols into their spell candles, anointing their magickal tools with the sign's corresponding oil, wearing their corresponding colors, or performing spell work under the influence of the desired sign.

Our ruling planets are our celestial guides. Zodiac signs are static, but ruling planets are always on the move. The assignment of these planets goes back to the most ancient astrology texts and was already ancient knowledge, even then.

Aries is ruled by Mars. Aries is the first sign of the zodiac. Mars is aggressive, focused, not unlike the first sudden blooms of spring. Energy for plowing fields, new projects, new concepts, and growth, growth, growth!

Taurus and Libra are co-ruled by Venus traditionally. There is now a suggestion that Taurus is ruled by Ceres. Both signs are enthralled by art, music, beauty, and literature, which are associated with Venus. Taurus is more fixed and collects beauty to surround itself. Ceres indicates growth and renewal very much reflective of spring and, through Libra, sees beauty and wants to reflect or mirror it, create it, and be it.

Gemini and Virgo are co-ruled by Mercury, the planet of communication. There is now a suggestion that Virgo is ruled by Chiron. Mercury is communication and growth through interaction. Both signs thrive on social connections, whether via personal connections or social media. Chiron also heals and promotes growth through technology and science, as well as libraries and Internet search engines!

Cancer is ruled by the moon. The moon is ever-changing, with its rhythmic shifting through lunar phases. It provides emotional channels and stimulates the growth of harvest, family, and ideas.

Leo is ruled by the sun. Leos bring consciousness and ego to the table. Ego, not in a negative interpretation (unless aspects to the sun indicate it), but a sense of self and boundaries. Ego that ripens

---

* See the color chart in the Appendix.

Samhain—October 31

crops, ideas, and art in fulfillment of the seeds planted earlier in the season.

Scorpio is traditionally ruled by Mars and, in more modern times, by Pluto. Mars is represented by the tendency to want to get to the heart of any matter through action, while Pluto, however, likes to get there through analysis, through the underworld of personality and thought.

Sagittarius is ruled by Jupiter, the planet of expansion. A thought is just a concept and, unless released, it will remain unfulfilled. Jupiter takes Sagittarius's will and frees it to think, create, and project the concepts out of the self to the world.

Capricorn is ruled by Saturn. Saturn, rather than being a taskmaster, is a more structured and channeled teacher. Saturn lets us find growth and creativity by limitations, by creating with what we have and not what we want.

Aquarius is traditionally ruled by Saturn, while in modern times, Uranus is considered its ruler. Uranus wants to transcend global knowledge to universal knowledge. Uranus wants to show the world something much larger than itself.

Pisces was ruled by Jupiter in older times. Now, with the discovery of Neptune, it becomes more at home with deep thought, feelings, and the mystery of what's behind the veil of dreams, illusions, and life. While Jupiter expanded on dreams, Neptune makes them, giving them life and possibility.

Cartomancy

From the 18th century until today, cartomancy has remained one of the most popular forms of divination: the art of reading fortunes through cards. Within cartomancy, tarot is currently king in many countries, but cartomancy using standard playing cards was incredibly common in years gone by. In France, the thirty-two-card piquet stripped deck was commonly used for card readings, although a fifty-two-card deck can also be used.

Just like with tarot decks, playing-card decks contain four suits, and each suit has a specific meaning. Spades, which correspond to the tarot's swords suit, represent conflict, challenges, setbacks, and secrets. Hearts signify love, the home, intuition, emotions, and romantic feelings. Clubs are all about positive happenings, communication, and creativity, and diamonds represent finances, success, recognition, and rewards.

Before using the deck, you should do a cleansing to remove any negative energy attached to it. You can do this by running the deck through sacred smoke, clearing with crystals, or simply doing a visualization and cleansing with the white light.

Once the cards have been cleansed, hold the deck in your hands, and send your energy into the cards, and then ask your questions. Shuffle the deck and the card on the top will have the information you need to hear.

Great-Grandma Sophie was the only witch in the family, but my Grandma Grace, on the other side of the family, was, let's just say, "metaphysically inclined," but I didn't know about it until I was an adult. She lived in Washington state and, as a child, I didn't see her on a regular basis.

She became very spiritual after her husband died and, when paranormal things started happening in the house shortly after, she began looking for answers. Aside from seances and automatic writing, she read playing cards. Eventually I was sent all of her automatic writings and with it came her deck of playing cards that she used to read for herself and friends.

The deck is dog-eared and the meanings of each card, which she wrote on them, have almost faded away, but they were legible enough that I could strain my eyes and jot down what she wrote. There's only one card missing from the deck and that's the Ace of Spades.

This deck was created at least fifty years ago, and the messages are quite simple.

Samhain—October 31

Grandma Grace's Playing-Card Deck

Hearts: Emotions, feelings, love, and family

- Ace of Hearts: Wishes come true, health, and happiness

- 2 of Hearts: What you are waiting for will come to pass in two days

- 3 of Hearts: A trifling present

- 4 of Hearts: An offer of marriage

- 5 of Hearts: A long visit with your sweetheart

- 6 of Hearts: A wedding, extraordinary occurrences

- 7 of Hearts: Present from one who loves you, visitors

- 8 of Hearts: Flirtation with a stranger, journey across the ocean

- 9 of Hearts: Good time at entertainment or party

- 10 of Hearts: Love, power, good luck, and great happiness

- Jack of Hearts: A good young man, possibly a close friend, he tends to be a bit indolent

- Queen of Hearts: A woman who is fair and with jolly disposition

- King of Hearts: A man who is fair, considerate, and gives good advice

Clubs: Action, creativity, luck, wealth, and health

- Ace of Clubs: Good news about money

- 2 of Clubs: Things will change quite soon, obstacles

- 3 of Clubs: Telegram or telephone message

- 4 of Clubs: Business affairs, be careful of deceit and betrayal

- 5 of Clubs: Conversation about work, help is around you

- 6 of Clubs: A good friend, prosperity

- 7 of Clubs: A journey by night, possible love trouble
- 8 of Clubs: Plenty of work to do, troubles and jealousy
- 9 of Clubs: A long journey, an admirer
- 10 of Clubs: A card of good business, financial success
- Jack of Clubs: Dark-haired. A student, industrious, a reliable friend
- Queen of Clubs: Dark-haired, society women, very self-confident
- King of Clubs: Dark-haired man, honest, affectionate, and generous

Diamonds: Practicalities, energy, money, and courage

- Ace of Diamonds: A letter or a message
- 2 of Diamonds: Two weeks or two months, perhaps a new business partnership
- 3 of Diamonds: An engagement ring, beware of arguments
- 4 of Diamonds: A present, unexpected money
- 5 of Diamonds: Health and wealth, possible birth of a child
- 6 of Diamonds: A check coming to you
- 7 of Diamonds: A journey by day, problem at work
- 8 of Diamonds: A meeting about money matters, new job or travel
- 9 of Diamonds: Pleasant surprises, new business opportunities
- 10 of Diamonds: Money, success, and financial stability
- Jack of Diamonds: A fair-haired youth, spends his money foolishly, sometimes dishonest and unreliable
- Queen of Diamonds: Fair hair, likes to party and gossip, and fond of dressing up

Samhain—October 31

- King of Diamonds: Very fair-haired man, he is influential and, at times, very stubborn, a man with money

Spades: Communicating, justice, death, and destiny

- Ace of Spades: Was missing in this deck (Traditional interpretations of the Ace of Spades include bad luck, death, or an ending.)
- 2 of Spades: A long time, probably a year of changes
- 3 of Spades: Tears, heartbreak in a relationship
- 4 of Spades: Someone is going to make you angry, small illness
- 5 of Spades: Gossips, things that seem to be standing in your way will turn out for the best
- 6 of Spades: A game of cards, things will start improving
- 7 of Spades: An accident on a journey, not serious
- 8 of Spades: You'll be receiving document or will

- 9 of Spades: Disappointment, stress, and anxiety

- 10 of Spades: There will be something to worry about

- Jack of Spades: A young, quick-tempered man with black hair

- Queen of Spades: A black-haired, divorced or widowed woman

- King of Spades: Dark hair, selfish older man with a very bad temper

Tim Shaw wears many hats in the metaphysical world. He is an esoteric seeker, spirit medium, teacher, and lecturer. He introduced me to scrying and crafted my first black mirror. I want to share his wisdom when it comes to the ancient art of scrying.

The Ancient Art of Scrying

by Tim Shaw

From the beginning of time, man has sought to foresee future events or communicate with an unseen world. There have been various methods practiced throughout the ages, however one in particular stands out as a being almost universal: the art of scrying. The art of scrying has come to us from the past as one of the oldest yet simplest forms of divination that has ever been used. When studying scrying, you will quickly find that it is as diverse as every tradition or culture in the world. Each method reflects an individual's belief system or ancestral history.

The *Oxford English Dictionary* defines the word "scry" as a truncated form of the French derivation of *descry* and of the Latin word *describe* which loosely means "to call out," "to catch sight of from a distance," and "to discover by observation." The *Merriam-Webster Dictionary* has a similar definition of "scry." It originates from the old French word *ascrye*, meaning to "to call out."

In today's world, scrying simply means the ability to foretell the future or communicate with the "other side" using a reflective object or surface. When humanity was in its hunter and gatherer stages of nomadic life, we needed help in locating safe shelter, fresh water, finding where the herds were, and, of course, the locations of competing tribes.

Samhain—October 31

A common method that was probably used by ancient man was to gaze into a calm pool of water. By doing this, they believed that the spirits would share the desired information. In most cases, it would be their own images that were seen reflected. This would have been interpreted as the images of their ancestors. Softening their focus, they might begin to see cloudy visions beyond the water's surface. After staring for a short time, the clouds would eventually clear, revealing far-off vistas or other knowledge that was important to the tribe's survival.

Today, we can now assume that the practice of scrying was not an isolated neolithic ritual. It has come to light that the Mayan culture used polished obsidian as a means of gazing and divination. Frescos that adorn the walls of the Villa of Mysteries in Pompeii may show a form of scrying. These depictions seem to show an initiate gazing into a copper or silver bowl. Currently, in many Pagan and magickal traditions, believers will stare at a highly polished metallic disc as an aid to foretell the future or communicate with guides and spirits.

Scrying was first used in an official government capacity during the reign of Queen Elizabeth I. Her personal philosopher, Dr. John Dee, was often consulted on many affairs of importance. Dr. Dee was a well-known mathematician, alchemist, royal astrologer, and seer. His assistant, Edward Kelley, was said to be especially skilled at scrying and would use a either a perfect crystal or a polished obsidian mirror to conduct his sessions. His preferred divination tool was named a *speculum* (not to be confused with the medical device of the same name). This highly polished black obsidian mirror may have originated in Mexico and been brought home as a gift for royalty. Dee, however, claimed that it had been given to him by angels. The artifact has now been preserved within the collection of the British Museum.

In Tibet, those practicing a form of scrying will sometimes gaze at their wetted thumbnail, which is made wet by licking, in order to perceive ancestral communication or visualize future events. The cunning folk of Ireland often use a blue glass bottle filled with water as a tool for scrying, such as in the practices of the legendary herbalist and bean-feasa Biddy Early. In the United States, the prophet Joseph Smith, founder of the Church of Jesus

Christ of Latter-Day Saints, was said to place special stones at the bottom of a white stovepipe hat. He then put his face into the hat, blocking out all light, to see visions. Smith used the stones to find treasure or gain special information.

Scrying can be practiced using an assortment of objects. The following are several of the more common types of methods:

Black mirror—A normal piece of glass where one side has been blackened, usually by painting the back

Cloud scrying—Watching for patterns in cloud formations that will form into meaningful symbols

Copper disc scrying—The use of a highly polished copper disc or bottom of a copper bowl that is gazed upon to gain esoteric knowledge or communication

Crystallomancy—The use of natural or highly polished crystals or polished glass

Hydatoscopy—Same as hydromancy, except specifically using rainwater

Hydromancy—Divination by scrying the surface of calm water

Smoke scrying—Interpreting the patterns of smoke produced by a fire

The Basic Method for Using a Black Mirror

The following are suggestions for the beginning diviner to attempt the practice of scrying:

Use spiritual protection—As with all rituals or working with tools of divination, some sort of form of spiritual protection should be included before and after each session.

Always set an intention—You must set a single goal or intention in order to achieve a good result. (Having too many questions will result in confusing visions or answers.)

Set a time limit—When beginning, set a soft-toned timer for ten minutes. If you do not get an impression or vision within that allotted time, then take a break and try again later. Some workers will see something immediately, while others need time to adjust and practice. Always remember that this is not a competition.

Samhain—October 31

How to Make a Black Mirror

You will need:

- Photo frame with glass
- Black gloss spray paint
- Newspaper

Use a photo frame that is pleasing to you. (I suggest thrift stores because the frames are inexpensive and you are repurposing an item.)

1. Disassemble the photograph frame, placing the glass on sheets of newspaper.
2. If you choose to clean the glass, do not use a commercial cleaner. This may cause problems with the paint. I suggest simply using a cotton cloth.
3. Spray one side of the glass. Let the paint dry.
4. Inspect the glass. If some areas appear lighter than others, re-spray the glass and let it dry.
5. Reassemble the frame with the painted side on the back.

Note: Some workers believe that the very best time to make a black mirror is during a waxing moon and that it should be empowered or programmed during a full moon. However, a tool of divination can be created at any time and still operate well.

6. Some workers will bless, consecrate, or program the mirror for the type or work that it is intended for (specifically for two-way spirit communication or foretelling the future, for example).

When using a black mirror or another upright polished object:

1. In a darkened location, stand the mirror upright upon a table. The location must be dark in order to keep your focus upon the mirror's surface with little or no distractions. If there are lights in the room, turn them off.
2. Place a candle (real or battery-operated) behind you. The candle must not reflect onto the mirror itself. This will provide just enough light to

keep your focus upon the dark outline of the scrying tool that you are using.

3. Set an intention. Decide exactly what you wish to accomplish in this scrying session (seeing the future, spirit communication, and so forth). Say your intention out loud.

4. Taking four or five deep breaths, close your eyes for a count of ten, then slowly open them, focusing on the center of the mirror.

5. Allow yourself to feel drawn into the darkness until a vision begins. You may feel your attention drawn into the blackness below the surface of the item you are using as a scrying tool. Continue to take slow breaths throughout the session. Allow yourself to be open to whatever sensations or visions you may experience.

Note: You may receive messages objectively, meaning that you see something in the surface of the item, or subjectively, meaning through your mind's eye. Both are perfectly acceptable. Many beginners report seeing a "mist" or "clouds." This is perfectly natural and has been interpreted by some workers as the piercing of the veil.

Be aware that the information that comes through might not be literal. Some communication may be conveyed in the form of symbols. To better understand symbols, decide beforehand on several easy-to-remember symbols that will help you interpret the information. (For example: an apple basket as a symbol of finances. Apples (or money) go into the basket and apples (or money) are paid out. Pay attention to the numbers of apples as that can indicate a small or large amount of financial payout.)

6. Eventually the visions will fade. This is a sign that it is the appropriate time to end the session. (Never attempt to stay focused or work once the visions fade.) Close your eyes and take several deep breaths, which will help in centering and grounding yourself. Slowly become aware of your surroundings and reality.

7. Journal or record your experience.

Note: This technique will also work on non-black, normal reflective mirrors, and the smooth surfaces of stones.

Samhain—October 31

Scrying Using the Biddy Early Bottle Method

Bridget Ellen "Biddy" Early was born in 1798 in Faha Ridge, County Clare, Ireland. She was an Irish herbalist and a *bean-feasa* (meaning seer or wise-woman) who had a particularly fascinating life. She outlived four husbands, fought against the Church and the local police force, and was renowned for her herbal remedies. She healed people, animals, and even crops.

At some point during her lifetime, Biddy acquired a bottle that brought her even greater fame. She used the bottle to scry, staring into its liquid depths as she considered potential cures for those who sought her aid. To learn Biddy's famous scrying method, follow these steps.

1. Choose a smooth, dark-colored bottle that does not have raised lettering or labels.
2. Clean the bottle, making sure it's free of fingerprints or smudges.
3. Fill the bottle with water and cap it.
4. While sitting, place the bottle on your lap.
5. Focus upon the widest portion of the bottle.
6. Allow the edges of the bottle to become fuzzy and out of focus.
7. Follow the technique used in black-mirror scrying.

Water Scrying

1. Fill a dark-colored or copper bowl with water up to the edge.
2. Gaze into the bowl, allowing yourself to be drawn into its depths.
3. Follow the basic scrying technique used with black-mirror scrying.

No matter the item used there are two important attributes that all great diviners possess. These are patience and practice. Like any trade or skill, time will perfect the work that you are doing.

Samhain Spells
Ancestor Offerings

During autumn and Samhain, remember and honor your ancestors. Show your devotion and let them know that you remember them by giving them this offering.

You will need:

· Fallen autumn leaves

Gather as many autumn leaves as you wish. Then find a quiet place outdoors to bury the leaves as offerings. You can bury the leaves in your yard, in the forest, or anywhere suitable that you see fit.

Dig a hole, place the leaves in the hole, then cover them over and recite the following incantation:

> If it weren't for you, there would be no me.
> You're the branches on my family tree.
> A long time ago, your leaves did fall,
> But in my heart, you still stand tall.
> I realize this offering may be overdue.
> Accept it with love and a big thank you.
> So Mote It Be

Ring the Ancestor Bell

When Samhain comes around and the veil is the thinnest, it's the best time to communicate with spirit in general and the best season to reach out to your ancestors and let them know that they are remembered.

You will need:

· A small bell

· Photos of your ancestors (or if you don't have pictures, write their names)

· Frankincense, myrrh, nag champa, sandalwood, or spirit incense

Put the bell and your photos on the table or on your altar, light the incense, hold the bell in your hand, ring it three times, then repeat the following incantation:

> Dear ancestors who have gone before,
> You'll be in my heart forevermore.
> Grant me your love and light of protection,

And point me in the right direction.
You live in my soul, your blood in my veins.
Forever and always your memory remains.
So Mote It Be

Ring the bell three times more.

Jack-O'-Lantern Spell

There are lots of things that we use to protect our houses, like witch balls, watchdogs, or witch bottles, but when it comes around to Samhain, we can add another house protector in the form of our yearly jack-o'-lanterns.

You will need:

- A pumpkin

- A carving tool

Once you get the face or symbol of protection carved into your jack-o'-lantern, place the pumpkin on your porch or by your front door with a lit candle inside and recite this incantation:

Jack-o'-lantern shining bright,
Ward off evil on this night.
Negativity must be gone,
Keep us safe until the dawn.
When the light of day is here,
It will banish all the fear.
Thank you for being on our guard,
In the house and on the yard.
So Mote It Be

If you're going to keep the pumpkin for a few days, repeat the incantation whenever you light the candle.

Thirteen Wishes for Friday the 13th

Some people fear Friday the 13th. Some fear the number thirteen in general. On the other hand, many of us see Friday the 13th as a day of luck and a very good time to do a wishing spell like this one.

You will need:
- A white candle
- 3 sticks of your favorite incense
- 13 bay leaves
- A marker
- A fireproof dish or a small cauldron

Light the incense and the candle. Think about thirteen wishes you want to wish for, then write each wish on a bay leaf, and when you've got them all done, place them in the cauldron or bowl and repeat the following incantation:

> I wish I may, I wish I might,
> These are what I wish tonight.
> It would be greedy to ask for them all,
> One wish will be fine when you answer my call.
> Grant me the one that you think is best,
> There is plenty of time to ask for the rest.
> So Mote It Be

When a raven is near, magick is brewing

Samhain Renewal

Samhain is a good time to cast out anything that doesn't serve you anymore. New beginnings and renewal are just hours away. Do this on All Hallows' Eve.

You will need:

- A black candle
- A piece of paper
- A black pen
- A fireproof bowl (or if you're around a bonfire, that's even better)

Light the candle and repeat the following incantation:

> Fire lights paper, it all burns to ash.
> Those things that I banish will go out in a flash.
> I know my wishes are not unjust,
> So it's ashes to ashes, and dust to dust.
> So Mote It Be

Write what you want to get rid of on each small piece of paper, then hold it up to the candle flame. When it catches fire, drop it into the bowl, and say, "Begone."

If you're throwing it into a bonfire, you can put your wishes in a small paper bag and throw it into the fire all at once. That makes sure that one of the banishments won't fly away.

If you used a bowl, take the ashes outside. If there is a breeze, you can toss the ashes and let the wind carry it off. If the air is still, dig a hole somewhere it won't be disturbed and bury the ashes.

Always be sure to practice fire safety.

Spirit Guide Invocation

Many of us work with our spirit guide, but sometimes may need a specialist guide also. It's just like our primary doctors sending us off to a specialist. It's easy enough to call upon a spirit specialist and you don't have to wait for an approved referral. Whatever the subject you need help with, be it health, wealth, or anything in between, there is always a guide who can take care of your needs.

You will need:

- A small white candle

- Spirit guide incense or myrrh incense

- Quartz crystal

Light the candle and the incense, place the quartz crystal in your hand, and recite the following incantation:

> With love in my heart and good intention,
> I call upon this special guide for an intervention.
> I need your help to guide me through,
> And teach me the right things that I need to do.
> Your sage advice is what I need,
> And I will follow as you take the lead.
> So Mote It Be

Put the crystal between the candle and incense and let them burn out.

New Wand Blessing

It seems like there's a national day for everything under the sun, including magick wands. National Magick Wand Day is November 3rd. When you get a new wand, it becomes part of the family and needs a welcome blessing.

You will need:

- Your new wand

After you have cleansed and consecrated it, sit comfortably, and hold the wand in both your hands. Close your eyes, feel your energy going into the wand, and when you feel it's done, recite the following incantation:

> Precious tool, I cherish thee,
> I know you'll do your best for me.
> We're conjoined, we are one,
> Our journey now has just begun.
> So Mote It Be

You can use this blessing on any other new magickal tools that you acquire.

Samhain—October 31

Honor and Remember Candle Spell

Certain times of the year we honor and remember those who were in the military and fought for our freedom. When you light a candle, the message will be sent to let them know that they've not been forgotten. This is the perfect spell for Veteran's Day, which falls on November 11th.

You will need:

· A yellow or white candle

· A pin

Use the pin to etch the name(s) of the person(s) you want to remember into the candle. If you have nobody in particular, you can write something like, "For all who have given their lives to help us keep ours."

Light the candle and repeat the following incantation:

You fought for our country and paid a steep price.
It cost you the ultimate sacrifice.
But you've not been forgotten, and never will be.
You've helped us remain the land of the free.
Thanks for your service, and all that you gave.
It allows us to live in the home of the brave.
So Mote It Be

Leave the candle lit as long as you can, but never leave a lit candle unattended.

Voyager's Prayer for a Cherished Pet

We are born, we live, we love, and then we must depart. I think it's important that we let our little loved ones know that they will not be far away, that love never dies, and to send them off with love. Light a white candle and recite this prayer:

Your time has come, my little friend.
Your physical life is at its end.
As you cross over, do not fear.

Know that your spirit will always be near.
The bond of love will act as a tether,
And deep in our hearts we're always together.
When it's my turn, I'll see you there.
Together again, without a care.
With all my love, I set you free.
May your voyage be blissful.
So Mote It Be

Thanksgiving Spell of Appreciation

The American holiday of Thanksgiving falls annually on the fourth Thursday of November, in between the sabbats of Samhain and Yule. For that reason, I have inserted a Thanksgiving spell into this section devoted to the Samhain season.

Autumn is a busy time of year with much to do, so it's appropriate to cast a spell that's short and sweet, with no need for tools of any kind. This is a simple spoken spell that you can do when you have a minute or two. All you need to do is sit down, catch your breath, and repeat the following incantation:

Fire, water, earth, and air,
I thank the elements with this prayer.
I also thank Spirit, that guides me each day,
And carefully keeps me from going astray.
I appreciate both morning and night,
The sun and the moon and the stars that shine bright.
I'm thankful for loved ones, both living and gone,
And those close friends that I can call upon.
I thank the things that make me smile,
And even the frowns every once in a while.
There's so much more than I can say,
But I will leave that for another day.
So Mote It Be

Samhain—October 31

Tarot Motivation

No matter how exciting things might be in your life, sometimes we fall into a rut. This tarot spell should do the trick to get you back on track.

You will need:

- Ace of Wands (for inspiration)

- Judgment (for rebirth, inner calling)

- Strength (for confidence)

- Page of Wands (for inspiration)

- A stick of vanilla incense

Lay the cards down, light the incense, and recite the following incantation:

Take away this sluggish streak,
And reinforce the strength I seek.
Recently, I lost motivation,
I'll get it back with determination.
With these cards and my intent,
I will lose the discontent.
So Mote It Be

Let the incense burn out completely.

The Mirror of Perception

Mirrors reflect who we are. They are not judgmental, and they always tell the truth. Sometimes we like what we see and at other times, we don't want to look because we're afraid of what we might see. This spell has been created for those days you're feeling down. Gazing into a mirror allows you to confront your emotions and the reactions that go along with them. It's always necessary to come face-to-face with what's wrong before it can be made right. Trust yourself in what you see and your looking glass will become your ally instead of your enemy.

You will need:

- A mirror

- A tablespoon of sea salt

- 1 cup of water

- A soft hand towel

Cleanse the mirror by making a solution of a tablespoon of sea salt in a cup of water. When the salt dissolves, gently wipe the mirror with the soft cloth. When it dries, sit in front of the mirror, look at your reflection for a moment, and then recite the following incantation:

> Mirror, mirror, shining bright,
> I need your help to make things right.
> Please reflect your energy. That is the key,
> Open my eyes and let me see.
> Remind me that sometimes we fail,
> But in the end, we do prevail.
> Your radiance fills my body and soul,
> And I will not get out of control.
> The very next time I look upon thee,
> I know there will be a happier me.
> So Mote It Be

Some folks set aside a special mirror for spell work, but don't worry if you don't want to do that. Remember that your intention is what makes for a successful outcome.

Enchant Your Jewelry

Enchanting your jewelry just means that you are going to infuse it with magickal energy for a specific purpose. Depending on what you want it for, you can turn your jewelry pieces into amulets, charms, or talismans. Keep in mind what your intentions are and consider that each gemstone, metal, and sacred symbol will have its own meaning.

You will need:

- A piece of jewelry

- A white candle

Samhain—October 31

Find a quiet place and light the candle, then choose the power that you want the jewelry to acquire. Hold the jewelry in your hands, focus on your intention and pour your energy into it.

Hold on for a moment or two, then repeat the following incantation:

Enchanted object that I hold,
Allow your magick to unfold.
Feel the energy settling in.
From now on we play to win.
With my energy we will pursue
The intentions that I give to you.
So Mote It Be

Hold on to the piece of jewelry close to your heart for a few more moments, then blow out the candle.

Transform a Necklace into a Pendulum

Pendulums have been used in magick and divination for ages and ages. Using one is a very simple method to help enable someone to obtain information. A pendulum consists of a weighted object suspended from a pivot so that it can swing freely. It doesn't have to be elaborate, and there's no need to run out and buy one. All you need to do is open your jewelry box or look down at what you are wearing around your neck and see that you already have a pendulum, even if you didn't know it. It doesn't matter if it's a crystal, charm, amulet, or anything else; as long as it has a bit of weight to it, you're ready to go.

I have bought pendulums and some were given to me, but I don't usually carry any of them around with me because if I'm not at home and there is a need for me to use one, I just take off my necklace with my pentagram charm and it works perfectly.

Before you begin using your necklace pendulum, you will need to charge it. If you have time and are going to use that necklace all the time, you can cleanse and charge it the usual ways by sacred smoke, sea salt, moonlight, and the like. Another way that works very well is to put your own energy into it.

Magick for All Seasons

Take your necklace into your hands, close your eyes, and envision your energy flowing down your arms, into your hands, and into the charm itself. Maintain that vision for a minute or two.

Once that is done you need to calibrate your pendulum to see how it's working. The basic way to make a pendulum work is to hold the chain between the thumb and forefinger of your dominant hand. Allow the weight to hang freely. Make sure you keep it perfectly still. Stabilize your elbow by resting on something solid like a desk or a table and make sure your limbs aren't crossed.

Ask the pentacle to show you "*yes.*" When it starts moving, see if it starts moving side to side, forward to backward, or in a circle. Then ask it to show you "*no,*" and see which way it goes.

Ask it a couple of questions you already know the answer to, just to get used to seeing how it works. If you get kind of a weak movement and aren't quite sure if it's yes or no, ask it to please show you something bigger. If that doesn't work, start over and ask the question in a different way. If you still can't get an answer, perhaps it's because you're not supposed to know, so try another time or ask another question.

Creating an Ancestor Candle

We all have the power to communicate with our ancestors and we should. After all, we carry their physical and spiritual DNA, which is woven into the fabric of who we are. You can strengthen your connection to them by creating a candle in their honor. You can burn the candle on special dates like their birthdays or anniversaries or on Samhain.

You will need:

- One large white votive or pillar candle, or you can use a battery-operated (LED) candle

- Frankincense, myrrh, lavender, or sandalwood incense

- A pen with blue ink

- A piece of paper, ideally parchment paper

Samhain—October 31

• Optional: photographs or something that represents of the ancestors

Write the names of the ancestors you wish to honor on the parchment, but also add "And all others who have gone before" at the end as to not leave anyone out.

Set the candle on top of the paper, and if you have photos, put them around the candle. Light the incense and recite this prayer:

As the veil between our worlds has thinned,
I call upon those who have come before,
Those I have known and those who have been long gone.
Your blood runs through my veins, your spirit fills my heart,
And you will always live forever in my soul.
You live within me and will never be forgotten.
With this light, I honor your memory.
So Mote It Be

Birthday Blessing

Samhain is the witch's birthday of the year, but this spell works for any birthday. This is a unique gift for loved ones and friends, especially those who are difficult to buy for. It's not something you can wrap as a gift, but doing this birthday blessing for someone you care about lasts throughout the year.

You will need:

• A blank greeting card or, if you're crafty, make your own card

• A birthday candle of any kind

Light the candle and repeat the following incantation:

I light a candle for you today,
A birthday blessing is on the way.
You've made another trip 'round the sun,
A new journey awaits; the past is now done.
May love and prosperity knock at your door,

And all wishes be granted forevermore.
So Mote It Be

Copy this incantation on the blank greeting card, then blow out the candle and run the card through the candle smoke. Send or give the card to the one you've blessed.

Birthday Blessing Candle Spell

Birthday candles go back to ancient Greece when candles on a cake were offerings to their many gods and goddesses. In modern times, we make a silent wish on birthday candles in the hopes that it will come true. Do this spell for your own birthday or for someone else.

You will need:

- A small box of birthday candles

- A tiny cake, cupcake, donut, soft cookie, or pastry of your choice

The night before the birthday, place the candle or candles (as many as you want) in the pastry, then light them and repeat the following incantation:

Birthday candles shining bright,
Carry the wish I make tonight.
Tomorrow is [person's name]'s Natal Day,
So dispatch my desire without delay.
After I blow the candle out,
The wish will come true without a doubt.
So Mote It Be

Close your eyes, make a wish, and then blow out the candle. Watch the smoke rise, and as it goes up and away, say "Happy birthday" out loud.

Samhain Recipes

A Word about Recipes

A handful of recipes are sprinkled into each section of this book. Having written three cookbooks and having tried hundreds of recipes, I find

Samhain—October 31

the one thing that stands out about cooking is that some people think recipes are carved in stone. Well, they're not. Maybe as far as the cooking directions go, some rules are not to be broken, but that's not true when it comes to ingredients.

We all have preferences. If you find a recipe you'd like to try, but are allergic to or simply dislike one of the ingredients, get clever and alter it to your tastes. I promise that the kitchen spirits will not bother you or hold it against you if you do. In fact, some of those spirits are in spirit precisely because of food poisoning or allergies to an ingredient that a cook may have carelessly tossed in. If a recipe is problematic for any reason or even if you just think you can improve it, please feel free to tweak and change it. Have fun, be creative, and make food the way you like it!

Some of these recipes are short and easy, others will be longer and more complicated. Be adventurous! Try something new. You never know; you might find a new favorite dish, just brimming with culinary magick.

"The more you know, the more you can create.
There's no end to the imagination in the kitchen."

—Julia Child

Samhain Potato Casserole

One of the most important Celtic harvest traditions was that all the potatoes had to be dug up by Samhain. As such, it's a great night to eat potatoes. Mashed potatoes, potatoes gratin, diced potatoes, or roasted potatoes—odds are, you have a favorite way to eat spuds. There are hundreds of potato recipes, but one of my favorites is this potato casserole.

1 large onion, diced
2 tablespoons butter
2 cups grated raw potatoes
2 eggs, beaten
salt and pepper to taste
½ cup flour
½ teaspoon baking powder

¼ teaspoon garlic powder
⅛ pound of butter

In a saucepan, sauté the onions in butter until lightly browned.

In a bowl, mix the potatoes and eggs. Sift together the dry ingredients and add them to the potato mixture.

Stir in remaining butter and onions, then pour the ingredients into a one-quart casserole dish and bake at 350 degrees until the top is golden brown and the edges are crispy (about an hour). Serves four to six.

Spellbinding Sweet-and-Sour Cabbage Soup

This was my grandmother's favorite soup to make on a cold, rainy day, and it's perfect when wintery weather arrives (well, as wintery as it can get in southern California). It's one of the comfort foods from my childhood that I can't do without. I wouldn't be surprised if Great-Grandma Sophie made the same soup back in the old country.

2 pounds short ribs
1½ quarts water
1 diced onion
2 cups canned tomatoes
a small head cabbage, shredded
the juice of 2 lemons
¼ cup brown sugar
salt and pepper to taste

Bring the meat to a rapid boil in the water.

Skim off the scum. Add the onions and tomatoes. Bring again to a boil, lower the heat, and simmer for about two hours.

Add the cabbage to the soup, cover the pot, and simmer another thirty minutes, then add the lemon juice, brown sugar, salt, and pepper.

Simmer about ten minutes more. Taste and adjust the seasonings.

The amount of lemon juice and brown sugar in this sweet-and-sour soup will vary according to taste. Some prefer it sweeter, and others like it more on the tart side. Start with the amounts listed above and then add more or less of one or the other to suit your taste.

Samhain—October 31

Garlic-Onion Relish

I wouldn't suggest eating this relish if you have an important meeting the next day or are heading any place where you'll be in close contact with other people. This isn't a dish for the weak at heart or those with a delicate palate, but if you like onions and garlic, it goes great with a meal that's heavy on the meat, or you can use it as a condiment on burgers or steak. And if you're worried about vampires, don't be—this relish will keep them far away.

    1 cup olive oil
    3 tablespoons vinegar
    2 onions, thinly sliced
    2–3 cloves crushed or minced garlic to taste
    salt and pepper to taste
    anchovies and black olives for garnish

Mix the oil, vinegar, salt, and pepper. Pour the mixture over the onions and top with a few anchovies and black olives. Refrigerate until ready to use.

PART II

Yule—December 19–24

Winter is a magickal time of the year. With winter comes the traditional holiday season and all its bells and whistles.

Yule, the winter solstice, falls between December 19 and 24. It is the season of midwinter festivities, signaling the return of the sun and light. The god as sun child is reborn of the goddess. We honor the birth of life and the first hopeful glimmer of light that confirms renewal. Participating in the magick of Yule allows us to continue to be part of the turning of the Wheel of the Year. This time of joyousness is also a time to take a moment to reflect on the gifts of the goddess.

Symbolism: The winter solstice celebrates the symbolism of fire and light and is the longest night of the year. The day represents death and rebirth and a day of the sun's rebirth. We celebrate new beginnings, transformation, and the returning of the light.

Symbols: Evergreens, Yule log, Yule tree, mistletoe, holly wreaths, and bells

Activities: Decorate trees, gather greenery for the home, select a yule log, light bonfires or candles, make a Yule log. If you throw a sprig of holly onto your Yule log's fire, it will burn away your troubles from the past year.

Incense: Frankincense and myrrh, pine, cedar, bayberry, and cinnamon

Spell Work: Candle magick, cleansing spells, and shadow work

Deities: Brigid, Demeter, Odin, Diana, Chronos, and Ra

Gemstones: Ruby, bloodstone, garnet, emerald, snowflake obsidian, and clear quartz

Trees, Fruits, and Herbs: Clove, mint, chamomile, sage, nutmeg, apples, red currants, bayberry, mistletoe, and evergreen

Animals: Bear, boar, deer, eagle, owl, robin, squirrel, snow goose, sow, tiger, wren, snow fox, and dove

Colors: Red, green, white, and silver

What Is Your Birthstone?

Yule is a season of gift-giving. Birthstones, tailored to an individual's birthday, are among the most personal gifts one can give. You might think of birthstones as just another piece of jewelry, something of an astrological mood ring, but this practice has a long and magickal history. The custom of birthstones—the practice of assigning a specific precious stone to either a month or an astrological sign—dates back to ancient Babylon and India. Josephus, the 1st-century historian, believed that the origin of birthstones dates all the way back to antiquity and that the custom comes from the breastplate of the high priest Aaron, which contained twelve gems, each representing one of the Twelve Tribes of Israel.

Birthstones are also used for protection. It was a custom in Poland in the 18th century to wear one's birthstone as an amulet to ward off danger. In Hinduism, where there is a close link between birthstones and astrology, certain gems are recommended for wear on certain places on the body, depending on the individual's birth chart.

In 1870, Tiffany & Co., the celebrated jewelry company, published a series of poems that related each month of the Gregorian calendar to a particular gemstone. It wouldn't be until 1912, though, that the American National Association of Jewelers (now called Jewelers of America) officially adopted a standardized list of birthstones. The list was updated in 1952 by the Jewelry Industry Council of America, appointing alexandrite the birthstone for June, citrine for November, and pink tourmaline for October. December's birthstone, previously lapis lazuli, was replaced with diamond or zircon. (Tanzanite is another birthstone possibility for December, added by the American Gem Trade Association.)

Birthstone lore continues to evolve. In 2021, Japan added ten new birthstone alternatives—so if you don't like your assigned birthstone, look around. There may be plenty of options.

Below are the birthstones in a number of systems—traditional, modern, mystical, and Ayurvedic—to give you some inspiration and a little bit of gemstone magick.

January
> Modern: Garnet
> Traditional: Garnet
> Mystical: Emerald
> Ayurvedic: Garnet
> 15th-20th century: Garnet

February
> Modern: Amethyst
> Traditional: Amethyst
> Mystical: Bloodstone
> Ayurvedic: Amethyst
> 15th-20th century: Amethyst, hyacinth, pearl

March
> Modern: Aquamarine
> Traditional: Bloodstone
> Mystical: Jade
> Ayurvedic: Bloodstone
> 15th-20th century: Bloodstone, jasper

April
> Modern: Diamond
> Traditional: Diamond
> Mystical: Opal

Yule—December 19–24

Ayurvedic: Diamond
15th-20th century: Diamond, sapphire

May
Modern: Emerald
Traditional: Emerald
Mystical: Sapphire
Ayurvedic: Agate
15th-20th century: Agate, emerald

June
Modern: Pearl, moonstone
Traditional: Alexandrite
Mystical: Moonstone
Ayurvedic: Pearl
15th-20th century: Agate, cat's eye, turquoise

July
Modern: Ruby
Traditional: Ruby
Mystical: Ruby
Ayurvedic: Ruby
15th-20th century: Onyx, turquoise

August
Modern: Peridot
Traditional: Sardonyx
Mystical: Diamond
Ayurvedic: Sapphire
15th-20th century: Carnelian, moonstone, sardonyx, topaz

September
Modern: Sapphire
Traditional: Sapphire
Mystical: Agate

Ayurvedic: Moonstone
15th-20th century: Chrysolite

October
Modern: Opal, tourmaline
Traditional: Tourmaline
Mystical: Jasper
Ayurvedic: Opal
15th-20th century: Beryl, opal

November
Modern: Yellow topaz, citrine
Traditional: Citrine
Mystical: Pearl
Ayurvedic: Topaz
15th-20th century: Pearl, topaz

December
Modern: Blue topaz, turquoise, tanzanite
Traditional: Zircon, turquoise, lapis lazuli
Mystical: Onyx
Ayurvedic: Ruby
15th-20th century: Bloodstone, ruby

Zodiac Birthstones

Aries (March 21st-April 19th): Diamond
Taurus (April 20th-May 20th): Sapphire
Gemini (May 21st-June 20th): Agate
Cancer (June 21st-July 22nd): Emerald
Leo (July 23rd-August 22nd): Onyx
Virgo (August 23rd-September 22nd): Carnelian
Libra (September 23rd-October 22nd): Peridot
Scorpio (October 23rd-November 21st): Beryl
Sagittarius (November 22nd-December 21st): Topaz

Yule—December 19–24

Capricorn (December 22nd-January 19th): Ruby
Aquarius (January 20th-February 18th): Garnet
Pisces (February 19th-March 20th): Aquamarine

Birthday Stones

In addition to birthstones, there are also birthday stones. Birthday stones are assigned to each day of the week—so if you were born on a Sunday, your birthday stones are topaz and diamond. Try combining your birthstone and birthday stone in your everyday jewelry for extra luck, protection, and that extra bit of gemstone magick.

Sunday: Topaz, diamond
Monday: Pearl, quartz crystal
Tuesday: Ruby, emerald
Wednesday: Amethyst, lodestone
Thursday: Sapphire, carnelian
Friday: Emerald, cat's eye
Saturday: Turquoise, diamond

Yule Spells

Wish upon a Pinecone

Pinecones have been a symbol of eternal life, resurrection, and regeneration throughout human history. Like the Wheel of the Year, they represent the cycles of life. Wishing on a pinecone is a folk tradition that dates back for centuries.

You will need:

- Pen and paper

- Somewhere safe to light a fire—a fireplace, firepit, or a bonfire, for example (you can also do this in a large, firesafe pot, as long as you are careful and practice fire safety)

- A pinecone

Magick for All Seasons

Write your wish on the paper, then roll it up and place it in between the gaps of the pinecone. You can make as many wishes as you want, but all on separate papers. Once you're done, hold the pinecone in your hand and repeat the following incantation:

Fire, fire, burning bright,
I'm asking you with all your might,
Grant the need that I just willed,
Make my wish now be fulfilled.
I thank the tree from which you grew.
Please now make my wish come true.
So Mote It Be

Toss the pinecone into the fire and watch the smoke carry your requests up into the ether.

You can share this spell with others by inviting friends or family to take part as well. If there is more than one doing this spell, everyone should write their name on their wish.

Air Travel Protection

This is a time of year when a lot of people travel to see friends and family. In recent years, air travel has become more of a chore than a pleasure, but here is a quick and easy spell to help get you to your destination and back safely.

You will need:

- A stick of bayberry or coconut incense

- One feather

The night before you leave for the airport, light the incense, and pass the feather through the smoke several times while reciting the following incantation:

For my flight, I now prepare.
It's up off the runway and into the air.
May the heavens protect us in all kinds of weather,

And the plane remain safe and as light as a feather.
So Mote It Be

Pack the feather in your suitcase and have a nice flight.

Holiday Protection

Things get so busy when holidays come around and, in all the hustle and bustle, our defenses go down. Here's a spell to keep you safe from all the craziness of the season.

You will need:

· A quiet place to sit

It's really that simple. You can do this spell anywhere, anytime, as long as you have a little peace and quiet and a relaxing place to sit. Make yourself comfortable, relax your body, take a big, deep, cleansing breath, then repeat the following incantation:

May every evil eye upon me be closed.
May every tongue that speaks against me be silenced.
May every negative thought against me disappear.
May every bad intention return to sender.
So Mote It Be

Stay put for a few minutes enjoying the peace and quiet, and visualize your shields going back into place.

Cleansing Your Aura

Auras are an extension of our physical self, like a force field that is attuned to our health and emotions. Over time, our aura is exposed to an assortment of energies that can bog it down.

There are several ways of cleansing auras. You can meditate, use an herb bundle, or let the sunlight shine on you, just to name a few. The cleansing power of water not only can be used on the outside of our bodies, but it also has the power to purify our auras. Some people suggest that plunging yourself into a lake, river, ocean, or stream is best because nature's living water holds a deep power to purge the body and the soul of negativity, but you can get good results by taking a healing bath as well.

You will need:

- A few drops of eucalyptus or lavender essential oil

- A cup of Himalayan sea salt

- You can also add sage, bay leaves, lemongrass, or rose petals to the bath as well as other herbs and flowers of your choice.

Once your bath is prepared, step into the tub and recite the following incantation:

Sea salt wash away
Harmful energy from my aura this day.
Mother Nature's essential oil
Will certainly cease all turmoil.
Herbs and flowers will assist in the purge,
And a bright, shiny aura will then emerge.
So Mote It Be

Cinnamon Stick Candles

You will need:

- Plain white candles (they should be similar in size to the cinnamon sticks)

- Cinnamon sticks

- Scissors

- Elastic bands

- Twine or ribbon

If necessary, trim the candle or cinnamon sticks so that they are approximately the same height.

Place an elastic band around the candle. Slip the cinnamon sticks in between the candle and the band. Decorate it all around with cinnamon sticks. Lift the candle up to test the cinnamon sticks and if any fall out of the band, place a few more around the circumference of the candle.

Place the twine, or ribbon, around the outside, covering the band. Cut the twine so that it is longer than the circumference of the candle, then knot it with a bow. You can secure everything with a hot-glue gun as an optional final touch if you feel like it's necessary. Place them around the home for extra holiday magick.

Clearing the Air in the Workplace

The best method for clearing a space that is weighed down with negativity is using an herb bundle to cleanse the area, but in the workplace, that may not always be an option. Perform this simple and effective candle spell instead.

You will need:

- A small white candle
- A sharp pin
- Frankincense, sandalwood, or myrrh oil

Etch this Thurisaz rune symbol into the candle with the pin.

Anoint the candle with the oil and place the candle on your desk or on a nearby counter. Light the candle and repeat the following words three times:

> White light and flame, cleanse this workplace from all
>   negativity.
> So Mote It Be

Let the candle burn down completely. As it burns, you should feel the atmosphere getting lighter.

Repeat as necessary.

Shut Up!

The holidays can bring unexpected hurt. This is a binding spell to use on a person who has hurt you or someone you care about through malicious words.

You will need:

- A picture of the offending person—the target of the spell

- Sticky tape

Take the tape and place it over the person's mouth in the picture. As you do, visualize in your mind that person's mouth taped shut. Once you see it, recite the following incantation:

Your words are harsh and nasty, too.
It's time to turn the tables on you.
Taping your mouth will set me free
From all the bad things you have said about me.
So Mote It Be

You can place the photo in a bowl of water, which you then put into your freezer. Keep it in your freezer just in case you might want to thaw that person out at some point. Alternatively, just toss it away with the rest of your garbage.

If you don't have a picture of the person, you can draw a picture of them and write their name across the top.

Sleep through the Night Meditation

The holidays often bring worries, leading to miserable, sleepless nights. You're tired, but there's too much going on in your mind to be able to settle down and relax. Here is an easy spell to calm the mind and relax the body.

Yule—December 19–24

You will need:

- Clary sage incense

- Soothing music playing quietly in the background

- A fluorite or green calcite crystal or other calming stone

Clary sage is excellent for reversing the effects of restlessness, both physical and mental. If you cannot find clary sage, you could substitute with lavender or chamomile incense instead.

Turn on the music, light the incense, place the crystal under your pillow, crawl under the covers, and repeat the following incantation:

The sun has set, the moon is bright,
Now's the time to say good night.
My eyelids are heavy, the sandman is near,
It's time for my mind to be free and clear.
Let me sleep peacefully all through the night,
And wake up refreshed in the warmth of daylight.
So Mote It Be

Warding Off the Evil Eye

It is believed in many cultures that the evil eye casts misfortune upon people. Some may dismiss it as mere superstition, but others strongly believe in it and fear the power of the evil eye. There are a variety of ways to ward it off. For instance, if you think that someone has cast the evil eye in your direction, make a witch ball. They are designed to ward off evil eyes and other misfortunes.

You will need:

- A clear Christmas tree ornament

- Silver glitter

- Tiny quartz crystal and/or carnelian, black tourmaline, amethyst, and citrine

- Combination of spices like cinnamon stick, dried rose petals, rosemary, sea salt, oregano, dill, bay leaf, cloves, and mint
- Copal, frankincense, myrrh, white sage, palo santo, or sandalwood incense, either powdered or stick
- A picture of the Eye of Horus
- Optional: A religious medal of your choice

Remove the metal cap and hanger from the ornament. Carefully fill the ball with the above ingredients. As you assemble the ball, think about the protective energy you are trying to create and imagine it glowing with mesmerizing powers, ready to draw in whatever negative vibes are out there. Imagine the ball as your protector, helping keep you and your home safe.

Once you've got all the ingredients in the ball, put the metal cap back on. Make sure it's on snugly. Depending on the size of the hole on top of the cap, use strong red thread or a red ribbon to hang it. Once that's done, take the ball into your hands and repeat the following incantation:

May this ball banish the evil eye
And any negativity that might be passing by.
It will maintain its power when needed to disarm
Any curse or evil eye that could be doing harm.
So Mote It Be

Throw the Snow!

When there seems to be plenty of snow to work with and you can't make it stop falling, you can use it to your benefit to figuratively toss away things that might be troubling you. This could be bad habits that you need to get rid of or obstacles that are keeping you from obtaining a goal.

You will need:

- Snow. Just snow!

You can create as many snowballs as you need to cover everything you want to banish. As you form each snowball, see yourself placing that problem firmly inside the ball. Then one by one, toss the snowballs as far as you can throw them and repeat the following incantation:

> These orbs of ice I'm throwing away
> Will start ridding problems this very day.
> As these balls fly out of sight,
> Make all that's wrong go back to right.
> So Mote It Be

Relieve Depression

There's no getting around it. In the depths of winter, it's easy to feel blue. Sometimes we feel sad or depressed and need a little candle spell to help lighten the load.

You will need:

- One yellow and one pink candle

Sit quietly in a place where you won't be disturbed for a few minutes, then light the candle and repeat the following incantation:

> As I sit quietly here,
> I allow myself to shed a tear.
> A deep breath in, an exhale out.
> Pretty soon I'll be up and about.
> As the tears roll down my cheek,
> I feel relief that I wish to seek.
> It will not happen in one day,
> But being patient is sure to pay.
> Day to day from dark to bright,
> I'll feel much better in the light.
> So Mote It Be

Blow out the candles and watch the sacred smoke rise up into the ether.

Please note that this spell is not a substitute for seeking professional medical help.

Get Well Healing Spell

There are times we feel helpless, such as when we or someone we know becomes ill, whether it be simply an annoying cold or something more serious. But luckily there is something we can do to try and assist in the healing process with a visualization spell.

You will need:

- A white candle

Light the candle, then repeat this incantation before you begin the visualization:

> In my mind's eye I will look to find
> The malady that has health declined.
> And when I find it, my focus will be
> To envision it healed and hence worry-free.
> With all my heart and this strong intervention,
> Feeling better is my intention.
> I'll do my best to make it be gone,
> And see health improve from this moment on.
> So Mote It Be

Take a few cleansing breaths, then close your eyes and focus on the part of the body that is affected. For example, if there is a broken bone that needs healing, envision the break, and put it back together. If it's a chest cold, clear the lungs. You can also cover all bases by surrounding the body with a bright white, healing light.

When you're done, blow out the candle, gather the smoke between your palms, then open your hands with palms towards the sky and send your intentions up to the universe.

Repeat as needed. Remember, this is not a substitute for seeking professional medical help when necessary.

Leave the Year Behind

When the New Year is getting closer, that's when it's time to reflect on the past year and decide what excess baggage you don't want to take with you

Yule—December 19–24

into next year. This spell will free you of those negative people, situations, or things that have been dragging you down and you can start fresh.

You will need:

- A red candle for energy
- A blue candle for tapping into truth, peace, and protection
- A white candle for cleansing, new beginnings, and fresh starts
- A cinnamon stick incense for success and prosperity
- Paper
- A pen with blue ink

Sit down in a quiet place where you can reflect on those things that have been weighing you down and need to go. Write them down. Light the incense, then place the candles next to your list, light the candles, and repeat the following incantation:

I release the past and cut the cord
Of negativity I have stored.
Starting today I won't carry those ties,
From this moment on I've said my goodbyes.
I'll end this year with a clean slate,
And a happier new year I shall create.
So Mote It Be

Sit quietly for a moment and take a couple of cleansing breaths, then rip up your list and throw it in the trash. Blow out the candles, rub your hands together with the smoke, then open your hands, palms up, and send all that has been weighing you down into the ether.

Relax! The Holidays Are Over

The first week of the year is usually a letdown after the hustle and bustle of the holiday season. It's sometimes difficult to get rid of the stress and anxiety that came with the past few weeks, and one way to unwind and get rid of the stress is aromatherapy. Personally, I love walking into candle shops because the aroma of all the mixed scents is so wonderful, and every time I open my incense drawer, the scent of all the entwined incenses relaxes me right away. This incense potpourri spell will definitely take the stress right away.

You will need:

- 2 sticks each of your favorite incense

- An incense burner

Light the incense and let the fragrances fill the room. As you breathe in the sweet smell, concentrate on your intention of relaxing and leaving the stress behind. Repeat the following incantation:

> This joyful scent that fills the room
> Smells to me like sweet perfume.
> With each breath I will then seize
> A feeling that I'm now at ease.
> So Mote It Be

Yule Recipes
Wassail

Wassail is a festive holiday beverage traditionally made from hot mulled cider or wine. It's the perfect thing to drink on a long winter's night. Enjoy my recipe for wassail below.

1 gallon apple cider
2 cups orange juice
1 cup lemon juice
½ cup sugar
2 teaspoons cinnamon
1 teaspoon cloves
1 teaspoon nutmeg
½ cup brandy, optional
1 sliced orange

Yule—December 19–24

Mix juices, sugar, and seasonings together. Add the brandy at this point to make alcoholic wassail. Omit the brandy to keep this drink alcohol free.

Slowly bring to a boil in a large saucepan or pot. Boil for one minute. Reduce the heat and simmer for thirty minutes. Serve hot with sliced oranges floating in the punch bowl.

Fiendishly Good Black-Eyed Pea Salad

Some people say black-eyed peas taste like dirt, but since I've never tasted dirt, I can't agree or disagree. All I know is that I love them, and this recipe is so simple, too. Black-eyed peas are especially lucky to eat at the New Year. The traditional American black-eyed pea New Year dish is Hoppin' John, but if you're in the mood for something new, this salad is a wonderful alternative to serve at your New Year's Day brunch.

> ½ pound black-eyed peas, soaked overnight and drained
> 4 green onions, chopped
> ¼ cup olive oil
> ⅛ cup white wine vinegar
> 2 tablespoons lemon juice
> Tabasco to taste
> salt and pepper to taste

Cook the black-eyed peas in fresh water until they are tender but firm, about forty-five minutes. Drain.

Combine all ingredients, chill, and marinate for several hours in the refrigerator before serving.

Serves four.

If you'd prefer to use canned black-eyed peas, drain all the liquid and rinse the beans before you add the rest of the ingredients. Adjust the cooking time to about ten minutes.

Medieval Yuletide Recipes

I know most every family has the same menu for Yule every year. It's tradition. Many people have either turkey or ham along with a wide variety of traditional family dishes, passed down from generation to generation.

But it wouldn't hurt to try one or two of these very old recipes that were tradition back in medieval times.

These ancient recipes are not personal family recipes. They've been collected over the years from old cookbooks and such, so if they don't sound like those recipes your grandmother made, well, that's just because they came from a different granny.

Ginger Wine

Ginger wine is a fortified wine fermented from a blend of ground ginger root and raisins. Ginger is very warming, so it's a perfect drink for a cold Yule's night.

This recipe I've acquired dates to 15th-century England, specifically to the region of Cornwall. During the Dark Ages, as well as during medieval times, many throughout the Cornish countryside would have enjoyed this drink during a feast or village celebration, especially during the winter months, as it would heat up the stomach and prepare one for a hearty meal. It was also a choice wine to be used for the winter solstice, as its color denoted the season and the warmth it provided offered reassurance of surviving the winter ahead.

To make a ginger wine, you will need the following ingredients:

2 gallons spring water
1 pint brandy
1 large ginger root (peeled, washed, and sliced thin)
10 cups sugar (refined or raw)
12 lemons
3 ounces fresh yeast
½ cup red currants or raisins

In a large glass or stainless steel pot, bring the water to a boil. Add in the sugar while stirring constantly.

Add in the peeled and sliced ginger, and gently boil the contents for twenty minutes. Peel and slice the lemons into one-half-inch slices. Set aside. Add the lemon rinds to the mixture and then turn off heat and let it cool.

Yule—December 19–24

When the mixture has completely cooled, add in the lemon slices and the red currants. Stir to combine.

Add in the yeast and stir until totally dissolved.

Once completely mixed, add the liquid to clean wine bottles, or to make the finished product look truly authentic, use glass demijohns or carboys to store and serve from.

Preferably, let the mixture rest in the refrigerator on its side and with a cork in it for about one to two weeks so that it can ferment properly. When ready, add in the brandy, pour through a sieve or cheesecloth into wine glasses, and serve cold. Serves five to eight.

Buttered Beer

Perhaps this was the inspiration for Butterbeer in the Harry Potter series. However, unlike that literary beverage, this recipe contains alcohol and is not on the menu at Hogwarts. (But who knows? Maybe our brew is available at The Leaky Cauldron.)

12 ounces of beer
1 egg yolk
¼ cup sugar
$\frac{1}{16}$ teaspoon nutmeg
$\frac{1}{16}$ teaspoon cloves
$\frac{1}{16}$ teaspoon ginger
2 tablespoons butter

Put the egg yolk into a saucepan and slowly whisk in beer. Add sugar and spices. Heat over medium-high heat until mixture just starts to come to a boil. Remove from heat, add butter, and whisk until mixed. Serve hot.

Chestnut Soup

You can do more with chestnuts than roast them on an open fire. This soup is a beloved dish that originated in Europe, where chestnuts are abundant. It has a long history and is particularly popular in countries like France and Italy. It is a comforting and satisfying meal, especially during the autumn and winter seasons.

3 tablespoons butter
2 onions, thinly sliced
2 carrots, diced
1 cinnamon stick
2 pounds chestnuts, peeled
6 cups chicken stock
⅛ tablespoon mace
⅛ tablespoon nutmeg
salt and pepper to taste
1 cup heavy cream

Melt the butter. Add the onion, carrot, and cinnamon stick. Cover and cook until the vegetables are browned. Stir frequently to prevent burning. Remove cinnamon stick.

Blend in the chestnuts and stock. Cook until the chestnuts are tender, about fifteen to twenty minutes.

Puree in a blender. Return puree to the pot. Add seasonings and whisk in the cream. Keep warm but do not boil.

Mincemeat Pies

Mincemeat was originally developed more than five hundred years ago in England as a way of preserving meat without either the traditional salting or smoking. While they might not be as well known in other parts of the world, mince pies are still considered to be essential on British holiday tables, along with Christmas pudding and ham or turkey.

This pie is a remnant of a medieval tradition of spiced meat dishes. These dishes have survived the test of time partly due to their association with Yule. If you have access to minced mutton, try making a pie with it! It's a traditional filling and makes a wonderful pie.

Today, when someone says "mince pie," what most people picture is a dessert pie filled with chopped fruit and nuts. Historically, "minced" pie and its progeny, mincemeat pie, began as a main-course dish stuffed with more meat than fruit. As fruits and spices became more plentiful in the 17th century, the filling of these festive pies evolved.

Yule—December 19–24

Mincemeat Filling

- 2 pounds lean stew meat (venison or beef)
- 1½ cups suet or shortening
- 4 cups apples, peeled, cored, and chopped
- 2½ cups raisins
- 1½ cups currants, chopped
- 2½ cups sugar
- 3 cups pie cherries, pitted
- 1½ pints strong cold coffee
- 1 pint cider
- 2 teaspoons cinnamon
- 1 teaspoon nutmeg
- 6 teaspoons salt
- ½ teaspoon cloves
- 1 tablespoon mace
- 1 tablespoon allspice

Cook the meat until tender. You can use various methods—a pressure cooker works well to create tender stew meat, but if you don't have one, you can also use a slow cooker or roast it until tender. Set aside while you cook the other ingredients.

In large pan, add all ingredients except the meat and simmer for thirty minutes.

Add the meat and stir well to combine.

This recipe makes four quarts of mincemeat, which will fill several pies.

Pie Crust

You can certainly buy ready-made pie dough from the freezer section of your local grocery store, but there's something particularly magickal about making it yourself from scratch.

- 3½ cups all-purpose flour
- 1½ tablespoons granulated sugar
- 1 teaspoon salt

10 tablespoons cold unsalted butter, divided and cut in ½ inch cubes

5 ounces lard (substitute with butter or vegetable shortening if you prefer)

⅔ cup cold water

1 egg white

Combine the flour, sugar, and salt in a large mixing bowl and mix well. Add the butter and/or lard or shortening to the bowl. Using a stand mixer, hand mixer, or two knives, cut the butter into the flour until your mixture is crumbly (the crumbs should be pea-sized). Alternatively, you can use a food processor.

Add the water gradually, either by hand or by pulsing in a food processor until the dough holds together. To test, pinch a bit of the dough between your fingers. Wrap the dough in plastic wrap. Chill for at least thirty minutes.

Preheat your oven to 400 degrees Fahrenheit. Grease a muffin tin or mini-tart tins with butter, lard, or shortening. Separate two-thirds of the pie crust dough and roll it out onto a floured surface. You want it to be about a one-eighth inch thick. Taking a circular cookie cutter, cut circles out of the dough and press into the muffin tin or tart tins. Roll out the remaining third of dough to one-eighth inch thickness and make your pie lids. Here you can get creative! Make mini lattices, cut the dough into festive shapes like stars or trees, or any other fun shape.

Fill the bottom crusts with the mincemeat filling. Add the top crust or lattices and press the edges lightly together to seal them. Brush the top crust with the egg wash.

Bake the pies for ten to fifteen minutes. You want the crust to be golden brown.

You can store mincemeat pies in an airtight container in the refrigerator for up to four days.

Mincemeat pies are sometimes known as "crib pies." These pies were originally baked in rectangular cases meant to represent the infant Jesus's crib. The addition of cinnamon, cloves, and nutmeg was meant to symbolize the gifts bestowed upon Jesus by the three wise men. Like modern mince pies, these pies were small in size, intended to be hand pies. It's a common belief that it's lucky to eat one mince pie per day for each of the twelve days of Christmas.

Stuffed Dates in Honey

This sweet treat may sound like it came straight from an *Arabian Nights* tale, but recipes for stuffed dates actually originated in ancient Rome during the 5th century. Sugar wasn't used for sweetening during Roman times, and so the Romans instead relied heavily on honey, as well as other naturally sweet ingredients, such as dates.

In Greek mythology, the date is linked to the phoenix. It's said that the phoenix builds its nest in the fronds of the date palm tree. Every five hundred years, the phoenix catches fire and burns itself out before being reborn from its own ashes. Legend says that the date palm would also burn and be reborn from the ashes, making it a symbol of renewal and rebirth. If you're in need of a pick-me-up, a rejuvenating and delicious stuffed date might be just the thing to bring you back to life.

4 pounds dates, pitted
2 cups blanched almonds
2 cups honey
salt

Stuff each date with one almond and sprinkle with salt.

Place the stuffed dates in a baking pan, cover with honey, and bake at 325 degrees for fifteen minutes, stirring once halfway through.

Let rest until cool. Remove from any excess honey before serving.

Plum Pudding

"For we all like figgy pudding, so bring some out here! We won't go until we get some!"

The ultimate culmination of the traditional British Christmas banquet, plum pudding, also known as figgy pudding or Christmas pudding, is a type of pudding traditionally served at Yule. It has its origins in medieval England. Despite the name "plum pudding," the pudding doesn't actually contain plums. "Plums" is instead a pre-Victorian term for raisins.

Plum pudding is composed of dried fruits held together by egg and suet, sometimes moistened by treacle or molasses, and flavored with cinnamon, nutmeg, cloves, ginger, and other spices. It is aged for a month or even a year; the high alcohol content of the pudding prevents it from spoiling during this time.

You're going to want to make the plum pudding way ahead of time, if possible, because the longer it sits, the better it is. During that time, occasionally dribble the pudding with a shot of the spirits of your choice, like brandy, whisky, or bourbon.

1 cup all-purpose flour
4 teaspoons cinnamon
2 teaspoons allspice
2 teaspoons nutmeg
4 ounces chopped almonds
1 pound light brown sugar
24 ounces bread crumbs
1 pound butter or finely minced suet
3 pounds raisins (You can use a variety of dried fruit.)
1 grated apple
rind and juice of an orange and a lemon
8 ounces candied cherries or natural dried cherries
12 ounces candied fruit peel or candied pineapple chunks
10 eggs
1 pint of Guinness
5 tablespoons hard liquor

Mix all the dry ingredients together in a large bowl. Rub the raisins and other fruits with the flour and spices to give the plum pudding a nice texture.

Cut the butter into small pieces and fold into the dry ingredients.

Mix the wet ingredients in a separate bowl. When the liquids have been well combined, add them to the dry ingredients. Mix together. You want a somewhat loose batter, closer to a cake dough than a bread dough. If it's too dry, add more Guiness.

Line a heatproof bowl with parchment paper. Fill the bowl to within an inch of the top. Cover the batter with parchment paper. If your bowl has a lid, fit it on top of the parchment paper. If it doesn't, use tin foil. Use your favorite method to steam your plum pudding; you can steam it on the stovetop or use a slow cooker for convenience. Gently steam the pudding for at least twelve hours.

Remove the pudding from the heat and cool. When the pudding has cooled, remove it from the bowl. Gently dribble brandy (or any whiskey) over the top of it. Do this slowly, letting as much of the brandy sink in as possible. Seal the pudding in plastic wrap and then in aluminum foil. The aluminum foil should not touch the pudding directly as there is a reaction that dulls the foil and I suspect this is not good for the pudding or the people eating it.

Let the pudding sit for as long as possible before serving at Christmas or Yule. We are not talking about a few-hour process here; plum pudding can sit for months. Occasionally, take the pudding out of its wrapping and dribble the pudding with a shot of the alcohol you initially used.

The traditional way to prepare the pudding is to steam it again for an hour before serving. If you choose to do so, remove the pudding from its wrapper, put it in a bowl, and steam for an hour. However, you can also choose to make a hard sauce (recipe below). If you choose to make a hard sauce, turn the pudding onto a heatproof serving plate (this is very important) and, literally, light it up.

For some families, it's a tradition to put a coin in the pudding. Whoever gets the piece with the coin in it is destined for a lucky year! You can try it yourself with an oversized coin or, alternatively, serve chocolate coins alongside the plum pudding.

Hard Sauce
    2 sticks unsalted butter
    1 cup confectioner's sugar
    ½ cup brandy or whiskey

Soften the butter and beat with a hand or stand mixer until fluffy. Add your confectioner's sugar and continue mixing. The batter will change consistency.

When the sugar and butter have combined, slowly add the brandy. Continue beating until you have a light, fluffy mixture. Chill your butter-brandy mixture until firm.

When you're ready to light the pudding, pour a cup of brandy on top. You want to aim to have a small puddle of brandy around the pudding on the plate. This will light easily and you'll be treated to the beautiful sight of blue flames licking up the sides of your pudding! Hit the lights in the dining room and prepare to serve.

It is essential to practice fire safety if you choose to light your pudding! Do this only on a firesafe plate, on a surface that has no cloth, wood, or other flammable materials nearby. Likewise, when you go near the pudding, be sure any hair or loose clothing is secured and nowhere near the flame. Be cautious of burning your skin and be sure no children approach the cake unattended. The brandy is, of course, extremely flammable, so be sure there are no splatters of brandy around the firesafe plate that might catch and make sure you don't have any on your hands when you cut it. Whenever handling fire inside, make sure you have a fire extinguisher at the ready. A wonderful tradition can be ruined if not treated with the proper caution!

If you don't feel like lighting your brandy-soaked Christmas dessert on fire—completely understandable, if you're new to this tradition—you can also re-steam your pudding for a few minutes in the microwave.

Serve with the chilled brandy-butter.

Sugar Plums

They must be good or Tchaikovsky would have not written "The Dance of the Sugar Plum Fairies" in his *The Nutcracker Suite.*

Sugar plums date back to the 16th century when sugar was still a novelty in some places. Sugar was used as both a sweetener and preservative, and it was a great vehicle for creating treats using seeds, fruits, and nuts.

I think the idea of adding sugarplums to any holiday table is brilliant. This is a 17th-century recipe that is a bit labor intensive, but I've found that anything made from scratch with love tastes a lot better than something whipped together in five minutes in the microwave.

You will need:

1 pound of fresh plums

Plenty of sugar! You will need enough sugar to add a half-inch layer of sugar to the bottom of a large, nonreactive (meaning enamel or glass, not metal) pan, plus 1 cup of sugar for the syrup and enough for dredging at the end.

Wash the plums, halve them, and remove the pits. Add a half-inch layer of sugar to the bottom of a large pan. The pan needs to be big enough to contain the entire pound of fruit and then some.

Start layering fruit into the pan with the cut side down. After each layer is set in place, completely cover it with sugar.

Heat the pan, slowly dissolving the sugar, and bringing the mixture to a simmer. Remove the pan from the heat and set it aside to cool. Allow the fruit to steep in the sugar syrup, covered with a lid or tinfoil, for three days. Keep the fruit submerged in the syrup by adding a small dish or wire basket to the surface of the liquid.

Drain off the remaining sugar syrup and reheat it to a simmer. Reintroduce the fruit to the pan and poach it for one minute. Remove the pan from the heat. Cool and steep for three more days. Repeat the reheating process an additional time.

For the final, fourth treatment, follow the steps above, but add a cup of sugar to the syrup mixture this time, and cook the fruit for five minutes instead of one. Remove the fruit and drain the syrup. Rinse off any syrupy residue with water.

Dry the fruit on a wire rack, in the oven, or in a dehydrator.

Dredge in granulated sugar.

PART III

Imbolc—February 1

Also known by the Christian name of Candlemas, Imbolc is a Celtic fire festival. It's a time of reawakening, a lighting of the way to new hope as the earth heralds the beginning of spring. Even if you can't see it through the cover of white snow, we know the spring bulbs have sent runners into the earth, the ice floes on our lakes and rivers have begun to thin, and the first of the young animals due in spring have been born.

This is a season of cleansing and purification. It's a time to sow the seeds of our lives for the upcoming year and a holiday of preparedness. We scrub from floor to ceiling, bills are paid, and taxes are filed, so that none of the business of the winter interferes with the pure joy of the earth's rebirth.

Get rid of the things that may stand in the way of goals and prepare for initiation or rededication to a deeper spirituality. This sabbat honors Brigid, the goddess of inspiration, healing, and smithcraft, sacred wells, fire, and the hearth. Her inspiration leads us to truth. Her waters heal us and her flame burns in our hearts.

Symbols: Candles, lambs, bees, cauldron, chalice, cows, sheep, and swans

Activities: Spring cleaning, light red candles (red is the color of Imbolc), decorate your altar with fresh flowers, herbs, and symbols of Brigid

Incense: Amber, wisteria, violet, vanilla, and myrrh

Spell Work: Imbolc is a fire sabbat, the first fertility sabbat of the year, and is generally associated with cleansing and purification. It's an ideal time for purification by way of banishing and breaking hexes or curses.

Deities: Brigid, Aphrodite, Eros, and Hestia

Gemstones: Amethyst, bloodstone, garnet, ruby, and turquoise

Trees, Fruits, and Herbs: Heather, violet, basil, blackberries, and bay

Animals: Bear, deer, sheep, lamb, and cattle

Colors: White, rich green, and bright red

Plant Spirits in the Garden

I love working in the yard and spending time with the denizens of the garden. I'm especially fond of the lizards. These little reptiles are beneficial to any garden because they are bug eaters and enjoy dining on ants, aphids, and other pesky insects. When spring comes around, they come out of hibernation and are all over the place, basking on rocks, playfully

chasing each other up and down walls, and making sure I'm doing my share to keep the garden growing. I caught this little one peeping at me through the fence and assured him that I was doing my best.

Then there are the garden allies that we rarely see, if at all. Those are the guardians of Mother Earth. They are the faeries, pixies, gnomes, and the like. Gnomes prefer earthy spots, around trees or near water, pixies love being in a place where hummingbirds and dragonflies dwell, and fairies love being around flowers.

In addition to the elementals, let's not forget about plant spirits.

Some people believe that some things other than human beings can have spirits. Aristotle, one of the greatest philosophers who ever lived, was quoted as saying, "The soul is the principal of life." Hence, all living beings, from plants to humans, possess souls. Otherwise, they wouldn't be alive.

Every plant has a spirit and they have much wisdom to share, if only we are open to listen. Floriography, the language of flowers, has been around for thousands of years. Some form of floriography has been practiced in traditional cultures throughout Europe, Asia, and Africa.

Dating back to the Stone Age, plant-spirit shamanism has survived in the folklore, rituals, and spiritual teachings of many traditional healers. In modern times, the theory is that to be working with plants, you must go outside to meet your plant ally. They say that you don't need to look for it. Just take a walk and then listen for its call. It will find you.

I don't wait for them to find me. I go to them instead. When I get a plant from a nursery or, when I plant a seed, as soon as it pops out of the soil, I talk to the spirit and get acquainted.

If we treat plants with love, they flourish and grow, but in addition to watering and fertilizing, speaking to the plant's spirit can make a big difference. There is no right or wrong in communicating with the plant spirit unless you knowingly disrespect the plant or the spirit.

It's no more difficult to talk to plant spirits than to those spirits we usually talk to. For me, the main difference is that the spirits we usually talk to are not tangible. With a plant or flower, we can touch the leaves, petals, or bark. When a plant seems to be not doing well, we are able to touch the plant and send our healing energy into it. By touching a

Imbolc—February 1

thriving plant in general, we can send positive energy to it as well. Vibration of the voice also factors into the plant's welfare.

There was an experiment by the Smithsonian and NASA that showed that mild vibrations increase growth in plants while harsher, stronger vibrations have a negative effect. Research shows that positive vibrations improve communication and photosynthesis, which improves growth and the ability to fight infection.

Go outdoors, whether it's in your garden, a park, or anywhere else, and start talking to plant spirits. It's beneficial to both you and the plant, and if you keep an open mind and listen, you will be able to hear what they have to say.

Make an Ice Candle

Though this sabbat is a time to look forward toward spring, many places are still experiencing winter on February 1st. The elemental combination of fire and ice perfectly captures the spirit of Imbolc. Ice candles can be used for decoration and to wow any guests.

You will need:

- Herbs and flowers of your choice
- A large freezer-safe bowl
- A freezer-safe glass jar that fits inside the bowl
- Spring water or melted snow
- A gemstone of your choice
- A tea candle

Layer the bowl with your herbs and flowers. Fill the bowl about two-thirds of the way up with water. Then, place your gemstone inside the glass jar and place the jar into the center of the bowl. It should sink to the bottom.

If it's below freezing outside, put the bowl outdoors overnight, or, if you're in warmer climates, put it in the freezer.

When it hardens, let the bowl stand at room temperature for ten to fifteen minutes before trying to un-mold your ice lantern. If it's taking a long time, you can fill the jar on the inside of the bowl with some lukewarm water. When it is loose enough, carefully twist the jar and, once you remove it, slowly wiggle the ice lantern out of the bowl. Put a tea candle in the middle.

Use it immediately.

Creating Your Own Magick Spells

It's a simple matter to make up your own spells as you see fit. Some people even believe that the best type of spell is one that you have created yourself. Just remember that what you put into your magick is what you will get out of it.

When writing your spell, it can be as long or as short you want it to be. You can make it rhyme or not but be specific. If there is someone you are casting it on, make sure you mention the person's name, and to be on the safe side, say that this is spell is cast for this person only and will not affect anyone else in any way.

First and foremost is your intention. You must know that you have the power to enact change within you.

Use meditation to clear your mind of all outside influences before you get started. Remember that negativity within you can change magickal outputs in unexpected and unpleasant ways. Center yourself and keep a positive attitude while doing your spell work.

The next step is to focus on your goal, then look around and collect items that immediately remind you of that goal. You might want to enhance the spell's effect with an appropriate scent, gemstone, amulet, herb, or corresponding candle of the proper color. For example, a candle spell for money would require a green candle, a copper coin, or a green aventurine or tourmaline crystal. The number of accessories you use is up to you.

After you've gathered your accessories, prepare a sacred space and envision yourself surrounded by a bright white protective light.

Imbolc—February 1

You may also call on a deity, angel, or spirit guard to watch over you. If you want their assistance as well, you can use the phrase "By your power, through my will."

To invoke the archangels of the four quarters, say:

Before me stands Raphael, behind me stands Gabriel, at my right hand Michael, and at my left hand, Aurial. For about me shines the pentagram and above me shines the six-rayed star.

Go ahead and cast this spell, incorporating all your senses into it, and when you're finished, you must bind this spell. This is a realization that you take full responsibility for the spell and its intent because when you perform a spell the energy you have put into it is bound to you. By making the bonding statement, "So Mote It Be," you're acknowledging the power the spell has and you're solidifying your intention.

Thank the powers that you called upon, then ground yourself by sitting on the floor and taking a few cleansing breaths. Visualize small roots growing out of your feet and legs to anchor you to the earth. Stay put for a few minutes and enjoy the serenity.

Imbolc Spells

New Beginnings

Imbolc is a festival of lights and honoring the goddess Brigid. It's also the time to honor our own inner fire.

You will need:

- A white candle or a fireplace (if you're doing this indoors) or a fire pit or bonfire (outdoors)

Light the fire, then watch the flames as you visualize all the things that you want in this time of new beginnings. Take your time, and when you're ready, repeat the following incantation:

Goddess of the brightest fire,
Grant me the strength for what I desire.

The rite of spring shall soon be here,
And winter darkness will disappear.
These things that I ask will get rid of the strife,
So I can enjoy a stress-free life.
This fire ignites my fire within,
And a fresh, new cycle shall soon begin.
So Mote It Be

The Sky's the Limit Banishing Spell

New year, new you. If you want to get rid of a bad habit, a bad relationship, someone in your life, or anything else that's weighing you down, this banishing spell is quick and easy.

You will need:

- A biodegradable balloon

- A marker

Blow up the balloon, gently write your request or person's name on the balloon, and let it fly away while repeating this incantation:

Things have changed, I need you not.
This is not an afterthought.
It's time for you to now depart.
I'll not have any change of heart.
Up to the sky in the blink of an eye.
This will be your last goodbye.
Without you I can start anew,
Without your negative residue.
So Mote It Be

Refreshing Your Home

Even the cleanest house on the block needs a little boost every so often and this spell will help you get rid of any residual heaviness or negativity, both physically and metaphysically.

Imbolc—February 1

You will need:

- A broom or vacuum cleaner
- Lavender, palo santo, sandalwood, cedar, white sage, myrrh, or pine incense
- A sunny day

Light the incense in each room and repeat this incantation before you start cleaning:

> I'll clean each room from ceiling to floor,
> And send the past right out the door.
> The leftover heaviness that lurked about
> Is something we can do without.
> And when I'm done and the air is clear,
> Peace and calm shall reappear.
> So Mote It Be

When you're done cleaning, open the windows and let the house be filled with fresh air and sunshine.

Besom Blessing

Besoms, also called witches' brooms, are probably the most familiar and iconic item that is associated with witches. Nearly every famous Hollywood witch has a broom, from Hermione to the Wicked Witch of the West. Whether you make the broom yourself or have purchased it, a new broom coming into your home will need a welcome blessing.

You will need:

- A white candle
- Incense
- A small dish of water
- A pinch of salt
- Water

Light the candle and incense and repeat this incantation:

With sacred smoke and fire flame,
I welcome you with great acclaim.

Then put a pinch of sea salt in the water in the dish, sprinkle a bit of the salt water on the broom, and say:

Salt of the earth I give to thee.
Welcome home and Blessed Be.

Hold the broom close to you and say:

You are now a part of me and I'm a part of you.
United we will do great things together through and through.
So Mote It Be

Sweep Negativity Away

You don't need to use a witch's besom to sweep away negative energy. Any kind of broom will do. The difference is that the besom will sweep the air and the broom will sweep the floor.

You will need:

• A broom

• Dragon's blood, frankincense, myrrh, benzoin, or copal incense

Open the doors and windows so the negative energy has an outlet. Sweep all around each room and when you are doing that, recite the following incantation:

As I sweep around the room,
I dissipate all doom and gloom.
I send it back to whence it came,
And peacefulness I do reclaim.
So Mote It Be

When you're done sweeping, light the incense in each room to make sure the negativity doesn't try to sneak back in.

Imbolc—February 1

Unwanted-Energy Cleanse

Unless you're a hermit and never leave the house, we all pick up energy from people when we're out and about, and some of that energy can weigh us down, so here's a spell to get rid of that unwanted baggage. Because you don't know what you picked up from whom or when, all you need is your intention and your strong will.

Find a quiet place, and when you get comfortable, take three deep cleansing breaths, see in your mind that energy flying out of you like a flock of birds, and repeat this incantation:

> To the energy that isn't mine,
> Whether negative or benign,
> Leave now, do not stay.
> All your energy must go away.
> I have the power to make it so.
> Now it's time and you shall go.
> I am going to count to three and you'll be gone.
> So Mote It Be

Take three more cleansing breaths and you'll feel so much lighter.

Cleanse Your House with Sound

Loud noises have been used since ancient times as a method of clearing negativity. Mother Nature uses thunderstorms to clear the air, so to speak. Get a head start on your spring cleaning by sounding off, loud and clear, and rid your home of the harmful vibrations that may be lurking around.

You will need:

- A bell or just your two hands

After you've recited the following incantation, go from room to room ringing the bell or clapping your hands.

> The noise I make with bells or hands
> Is something negativity understands.
> Unhealthy energy now begone,

Your presence here must be withdrawn.
You need to return from whence you came.
I'm tired of your silly game.
It won't take long to be aware
That peace and calm will fill the air.
So Mote It Be

To complete the cleanse, you might want to consider putting wind chimes outside in the yard or near your front door to break up bad energy before it can sneak inside.

Lucky Saint Patrick's Day Candle Spell

Saint Patrick's Day falls on March 17th, between Imbolc and Ostara. It is an enchanted time, a day to begin transforming winter's dreams into summer's magick. You don't need to be Irish to have good luck. You can bless good luck on yourself with a simple incantation.

You will need:

- A green candle (or a white candle tied with a green ribbon)

- A sharp pin

- Clear quartz, tiger's eye, green jade, emerald, or peridot

- Cinnamon, copal, or jasmine incense

Etch the shape of a shamrock and the word "luck" into the candle with the pin.

Light the incense and the candle, hold the crystal in your hand, and recite the following incantation:

Health and happiness come my way,
Starting on Saint Patrick's Day.
Send sunbeams to warm me and moonbeams to charm,
And keep my loved ones free from harm.
May good luck be with me each morning and night,
And ensure that my outlook and future be bright.
So Mote It Be

Imbolc—February 1

Blow out the candle and rub the smoke between your palms, then open your hands with the palms up and send your message up into the ether. Repeat the spell as often as you like to reinforce the message.

An Easy Binding Spell

Binding spells restrain someone metaphysically, preventing them from doing something. It is often used to keep the individual from causing harm to themselves or others. This fairly common freezer spell is quite easy, but generally, this type of binding spell should be used only when no other methods have been tried to solve the problem.

You will need:

- Small piece of paper and pen

- A small freezer container

- Water

Write the name of the person you would like to freeze and write the action that caused you to do this spell. Fill the container with water and immerse the paper into the water. Close the container, then hold it in your hands and repeat the following incantation:

> You must be stopped from this day on.
> Your malintent will now be gone.
> I mean you no harm, it's my protection,
> To rid you now of our bad connection.
> In the freezer you must remain
> Until such time that I regain,
> The trust in you that that I have lost,
> But until then you shall not defrost.
> So Mote It Be

Put the container into your freezer and that's all it takes.

Reverse the Hex

If you feel like someone has put a hex on you, turn the tables and send it right back to them.

You will need:

- Vetiver, dragon's blood, or myrrh incense
- A sheet of paper
- A pen with black ink

Light the incense and visualize the hex doing a U-turn and flying back to its sender. Then write this incantation on the paper, saying each line out loud as you write it:

Now it is the time for me to take aim,
And return the hex from whence it came.
With all my strength I disable the attack,
And very gladly send it back.
May the bad intent that you wished upon me
Revert back to you.
So Mote It Be

Let the incense burn itself down. If you think there's a need, you may repeat this spell as often as you wish.

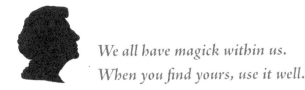

We all have magick within us.
When you find yours, use it well.

Just Walk Away Spell

There are times that you must rid yourself of certain people or situations but need a bit of magick to help you make a clean break. This walk away spell will do the trick.

You will need:

- A white candle

- Pen and a small piece of paper

- A teaspoon of sea salt

- A lemon

- Small bowl or plate

The lemon represents how your situation has soured and salt represents how it has become corrosive.

Light the candle and write the name or situation that you are going to walk away from and place it in the small bowl. Sprinkle the sea salt on top of the paper to cover what you wrote, then cut the lemon in half, squeeze the juice over the salt, and repeat the following incantation:

Things are not working out,
And now it's my time to depart.
It's over and done with no change of heart.
Drops of lemon and grains of salt will bring things to a close.
It's best we just walk away to get rid of the woes.
So Mote It Be

Sit for a moment, take a couple of deep cleansing breaths, and feel the burden lift off your shoulders. When you're ready, blow out the candle and toss the contents of the bowl into the trash.

Goodbye and Good Riddance Spell

There are people we need to get rid of in our lives for various reasons. They could be a friend, acquaintance, or someone you're emotionally involved with who is draining you dry. You know it's time to move on, but you're having difficulty letting go. A little bit of magick will always help you get things done.

You will need:

- Paper and a pen with black ink

- A black candle

- A fireproof bowl

Write the name of the person you need to let go of, then hold the paper in your hands and repeat the following incantation:

With this paper, I let go of the past.
It's now time for me to be free at long last.
I wish you no harm, but get out of my life.
You've given me nothing but heartache and strife.
So Mote It Be

Light the paper and drop it into the bowl. When the ashes have cooled, take them outside, throw them up in the air, and let the wind carry them away.

Torch Your Troubles

If you have a burning desire to get rid of your troubles, this spell can help you to fight fire with fire. This is a perfect spell for Imbolc.

You will need:

· A yellow candle

· Ylang-ylang or jasmine incense

· Pen with black ink and paper

· A heatproof bowl

Light the candle and incense then write down those things that are troubling you. Put the paper in the candle flame. When it catches fire, drop it into the fireproof bowl, and as it burns, recite this incantation:

Ashes to ashes, dust to dust.
Banishing problems is a must.
Fire burn brightly and take them away.
Please banish those troubles and keep them at bay.
So Mote It Be

When the paper turns to ash you can either take it outdoors and let the breeze carry it away or bury it in dirt. Blow out the candle but let the incense burn itself out.

Imbolc—February 1

Imbolc Recipes
Rosemary Salt

1 cup fresh rosemary leaves
1 cup coarse salt, like sea salt
3 cups kosher salt

Put the rosemary leaves and the coarse salt in a food processor and pulse it a few times until the rosemary and salt have been blended. It's going to be damp, and the texture should be like regular table salt.

Pour the kosher salt into a bowl and stir in the rosemary salt until it's totally blended. Then place it on a baking sheet and let it dry for a few hours.

When it's dry, store the salt in a jar with a tight lid. Rosemary salt is a fantastic way to add flavor to all kinds of savory dishes, such as roasts, soups, and stews.

Crepes to Charm

National Crepe Day is February 2nd. Most every country has something like a crepe. The French call it a crepe, in Jewish cooking it's a blintz, a *palacsinta* in Hungary, enchiladas in Mexico (crepes are both sweet and savory), and the list goes on. Make your own crepes at home and charm anyone who visits your kitchen.

3 eggs
1¼ cups flour
1 cup milk
½ cup cold water
1 teaspoon sugar
a pinch of salt
1½ teaspoons butter, melted
Oil of your choice

Combine all the ingredients in a blender and mix until smooth. Put it off to the side and let rest for at least an hour.

Brush a seven-inch or eight-inch frying pan lightly with the oil and heat over moderately high heat.

Pour in one tablespoon of the batter, quickly tilting the pan to cover it with a thin film.

Sauté for about one minute till the bottom turns brown, then flip it over for about half a minute, and then turn out to a plate. Repeat with the rest of the batter until there is no more, putting wax paper between each crepe. This recipe makes about twelve crepes.

Nut Filling

Conjure up a delicious chopped-nut filling for your crepes! If you're allergic to nuts, this spread also works wonderfully with dried chopped fruit.

> 1 cup chopped walnuts
> honey to taste, as well as to thicken the paste
> Milk, sufficient to create a spreadable paste. Start with a little
>   and add more as needed.

Blend the walnuts with the honey and milk to make a spreadable paste. Spread a little bit of the paste to taste over each crepe and fold the crepe in half. Serve immediately.

Sweet Spirit Angel Delight

This recipe comes from my friend, the late Kenny Kingston, widely known as the "Psychic to the Stars" (February 15, 1927-June 30, 2014). Not only did he teach me lots about the spirit world, he also showed me how to create some great recipes. He gave the recipe with his heart, and it will nourish the body and the soul.

For the Crust

> 1 cup flour
> 1 tablespoon sugar
> ½ cup margarine

Mix until just combined.

Press the mixture into the bottom (only) of a nine-inch by nine-inch baking dish and bake at 350 degrees for fifteen to twenty minutes.

For the Filling
> 1 can rhubarb
> 3 tablespoons flour
> ½ cup sugar
> 2 egg yolks
> ½ cup milk

Heat the rhubarb on a low heat. While it's warming up, mix together the other ingredients.

Beat the mixture until smooth, then add to the rhubarb and cook until thickened. Let it cool and then pour it into the pie crust.

For the Topping
> 2 egg whites
> ¼ teaspoon cream of tartar
> ½ cup sugar

Beat the egg whites with the cream of tartar until stiff peaks form, about four to five minutes with a hand or stand mixer on medium-high speed. Slowly add the sugar and beat until the mixture forms firm peaks, about two to three more minutes.

Cover the rhubarb with the meringue topping and bake at 300 degrees until brown on the top.

Cut into squares after it has cooled down a bit. Serve slightly warm or cool. As Kenny would say, "Enjoy it, sweet spirits."

Dragon-Eye Breakfast Sandwich

I'm guessing that back in medieval times, the flame that heated the skillet came from the neighborhood dragon, but a gas flame these days is a bit easier to work with. The fried egg in this breakfast sandwich looks just like the fiery eye of a ferocious dragon. It's sure to warm you up on a cold winter's morning.

> 1 tablespoon butter, margarine, or nonstick cooking spray
> 2 slices bread (your choice)
> 2 eggs

salt and pepper to taste
optional: maple syrup, jam, or honey

In a frying pan, melt the butter, margarine, or spray the pan with the nonstick spray.

Punch a hole out of the center of each piece of bread using a small drinking glass, then crack an egg into each hole.

Fry on medium heat until the bread is golden brown on the bottom, then flip the bread and fry till the other side is brown and the egg yolk is cooked the way you like it. Season to taste and serve with the syrup, jam, or honey.

PART IV

Ostara—March 19–22

Ostara coincides with the spring equinox. Earth has now awakened from her slumber, and while the day and night are equal, the light is gaining and life is gaining momentum. It takes place around the same time as the Christian Easter celebration and the Jewish celebration of Passover.

Spring equinox is a time for fertility and sowing seeds, and so nature's abundance goes a little wild. In medieval societies in Europe, the March hare was viewed as a major fertility symbol. This is a species of rabbit that is nocturnal most of the year, but in March when mating season begins, there are bunnies everywhere all day long. The female of the species is said to be able to conceive a second litter while still pregnant with a first. As if that weren't enough, the males tend to get frustrated when rebuffed by their mates and bounce around erratically when discouraged, which explains the old saying, "Mad as a March hare."

This is time of feasting and celebration. There is a sense of energy and promise in the air. This is when the clover appears in the fields, a symbol of the rebirth of the Maiden aspect of the Triple Goddess. (The Triple Goddess is typically envisioned as a trinity consisting of the Maiden, Mother, and Crone, representing the three stages of womanhood. These correspond to the waxing, full, and waning phases of the moon, widely considered to be the celestial body with dominion over women, especially their menstrual—and thus fertility—cycles.)

> **Symbols:** Eggs, rabbits, spring flowers, seeds, greenery, butterflies, and the sun and moon, representing balanced day and night, as well as divine harmony

Activities: Decorate eggs, plant seedlings, craft an herb sachet, set your intentions for spring, perform a house blessing, get fresh flowers in your home, do a garden blessing

Incense: Jasmine, frankincense, myrrh, dragon's blood, cinnamon, nutmeg, aloeswood, benzoin, musk, African violet, sage, strawberry, lotus, violet flowers, orange peel, and rose petals

Spell Work: Fertility, abundance, new beginnings, and cleansing

Deities: Ēostre, Persephone, and Flora

Gemstones: Green jasper, azurite, citrine, lapis lazuli, carnelian, tiger's eye, garnet, rose quartz, amazonite, and citrine

Plants and Herbs: Dandelion, lemon balm, mint, and orris root

Animals: Bee, butterfly, chicken, rabbit, ram, robin, and phoenix

Colors: Green, light blue, pink, silver, violet, white, and yellow

Creating and Working with Witch Bells

Bells have long been associated with warning and protection. They are an alarm or warning of impending danger.

Historically, people made bells from iron. In European folklore, it's believed that iron scares off, or at the very least agitates, fairies. People would not only use bells but also hang iron horseshoes over their doorways to ward off the fae and keep evil spirits away.

Bells have many uses in witchcraft. They are used in rituals; to clear and charge crystals; to invoke gods, goddesses, and the elements; and for protection. When hung on the door of your home, bells can bring positive energy, protection, and prosperity to the house and those who live there.

Witches' bells are easy to make. Using small- or medium-sized bells works best.

You can find the bells in any craft or department store. You also need metal rings, cords, or string. To personalize your bell, add charms

like feathers, beads, pendants, crystals, or whatever you have available. Cleanse them in sacred smoke (using incenses like sandalwood, myrrh, or sage).

Here are some uses for your witches' bells beside hanging them on the door:

- Ring your witches' bells to announce the start of a ritual or spell working.
- Hang them from your witches' cabinet or altar to ward off low-level spirits that may try to feed on the energy there and to warn you if someone is playing around with your sacred tools.
- You can also hang a bell from your pet's collar to know their whereabouts and to protect them from negative energy. (Make sure your pet cannot take the bell off or chew on it.)

- Hang them in your bedroom window, which helps ward off nightmares and trickster astral spirits.

- Wear bells on your body while dancing to raise energy and deter negative forces during invocation and rituals.

Here is an example of making witches' bells:
You will need:

- Bells

- Small hoop or wreath

- String

Pick out the kind of bells you would like to use. For your first time, I suggest little Christmas jingle bells. They have a place on top to thread the string, twine, or whatever you're using to hang them.

Depending on where you want to hang them, you can use as many bells as you wish.

Cut the pieces of string material into strips of different lengths and make sure they are long enough to be able to tie them to the hoop and still hang down.

Thread your string material through the bell until it is in the center of your string. Attach the ends to the hoop. You can make a knot or a loop, use a glue gun, or use whatever way suits you.

Jingle the bells and see how they sound. If you need more, add on. There's no right or wrong.

Find the place you want them and hang them up.

The Three Cs—Cleansing, Consecrating, and Charging Your Tools

It's important to clear your tools of all negativity and make them your own before you begin to use them, and Ostara—the time of spring—is a great time to renew your implements. Magickal tools can easily pick up negative energy in foreign environments. By using the three Cs, you remove or neutralize the energy and replace it with your own. There's no telling how many sets of hands picked your new tools up before they came to you and what kind of mood the handlers were in at the time.

Cleansing can be done in a variety of ways. You can use sacred smoke with incense that has purification properties, such as sage, pine, or sandalwood, or run the tool through sea salt, or place it outside in the direct sunlight or moonlight.

Consecration is an intention to make something holy. You're taking ordinary tools and turning them into sacred tools. By doing this, all negativity is instantly removed. Remember, your intention is the most important tool you will ever need. To do this, visualize a bright white light streaming down onto your tool. Ask your guardian spirit or guide to protect you and your tools from anything but the highest of energy forms and only to be used for the greater good.

Charging the tool is easy. Once it is cleansed and consecrated, direct your personal energy into it by holding the tool in your hands and sending it your power, spirit, and intention. Feel the energy flowing down your arms and into your hands and then out your fingertips and into the tool. By charging your tools, you will establish a tight personal link with them.

I like to bestow an offering to the new tools. This can be done in the form of a flower, a shell, a crystal, an amulet, or a charm. Always take good care of your tools and they will take good care of you.

Plant a Witch's Moon Garden

The idea of a moon garden is choosing plants of light shades that will reflect the light of the moon. Many blooming plants of white or silver give off an incandescent appearance in the moonlight. Some of those blooming flowers are moonflower, night-blooming cereus, angel's trumpet, Queeny White hollyhock, euphorbia, night phlox, tuberose, lamb's

Ostara—March 19–22

ears, silver sage, night-blooming jasmine, evening primrose, and lilac. Any white flower that blooms in the day will look beautiful under moonlight as well.

If you plant both annuals and perennials, you will keep your moon garden shining all year round.

The gardens can be of any size, and if you don't have a lot of ground space; you can always plant the flowers in containers and group them all together. Using white gravel in the garden will capture the effect of the light. You can also use solar lanterns, stake lights, or small LED lights.

If I must choose my favorite moon garden plant, I'd have to admit that I have always loved night-blooming cereus. The word "cereus" means it is a cactus, and most types of night-blooming cereus are fragrant. They can sometimes grow to ten feet tall!

The story behind my love of the plant goes like this:

I had two cereus plants growing on each side of the steps that lead up to my front porch. The plants were about six feet tall and when in bloom, there were dozens of flowers that opened each night. The flowers would open after sundown, and by dawn, were in the process of wilting. Their scent was very strong, and when I opened the front door, their fragrance filled the house with sweet perfume.

It is said that plants that bloom in darkness are symbols of the ability of beauty to emerge in dark times. That proved true one very sad evening, several years ago.

My elderly cat had just passed away. We called the vet and instead of having us wait until morning before bringing her in for cremation, he said someone was at the clinic overnight and he would let them know that we were coming.

My boyfriend gently wrapped her up in her favorite blanket and walked onto the porch, but for some reason, he stopped in front of the cereus and held the little one up to one of the blooming flowers. He said he wanted her to smell the sweetness of the flower one last time. That was a lovely gesture and I started to cry, but right then the biggest, furriest white moth as big as my hand came flying out of nowhere and began to flutter right over the cat in my boyfriend's arms. The moth circled several times, not afraid that we were there, then gently landed on the blanket right next to our fur baby's head for a moment and did a little dance before taking off into the night.

I don't know why that happened, but it almost looked as through the moth were performing some kind of ritual. I'd like to think that perhaps the moth was sent to collect my cat's soul. Every time I think of a moon garden, I remember the cereus and the most beautiful and gentlest moth I have ever seen.

Night pollinators, like nectar-feeding bats and night-feeding moths, are drawn to pale flowers and their fragrance. Make sure you choose a spot that can be viewed from a patio or porch or through a window from inside the house. If you're going through a rough time, go sit and look out at your moon garden. You might have a huge moth pay you a visit to show you that there is beauty in the darkness.

Ostara Spells
Seed Magick

Planting seeds at Ostara is celebrating the rebirth of Mother Earth.

You will need:

- Seeds of your choice

Whether you're planting just one indoor plant or are filling your outdoor space with new growth, communing with the plant spirits will ensure a happy garden. Be sure to follow the instructions on your packet of seeds.

Before you plant your seeds, sprouts, or seedlings, hold them in your hands and speak to the plant spirits by whispering words of encouragement to grow strong and beautiful, and promise that you will take good care of them.

Remember to get acquainted with the living beings that reside in your garden. Hang hummingbird feeders, grow plants that attract the bees and butterflies, and don't forget to leave offerings for the elementals that share your space.

Easter Egg Magick

Eggs have been used in magickal practices across countless cultures for thousands upon thousands of years. They are a symbol of fertility and a powerful symbol of protection because of their hard outer shell. Decorating eggs is a long-standing Easter tradition. Eggs are dipped in colorful dyes and decorated with all kinds of patterns. Unleash your creativity and use this magickal spell to convey your desires to the universe.

You will need:

- Hard-boiled eggs

- A wax crayon

- Easter egg dye

Use the crayon to write words of intention, sigils, or magickal symbols on your eggs before dying them. When coloring the eggs, choose the color that works hand-in-hand with your intention. If you have romantic intentions, for example, you might choose red or pink. For psychic intuition or wisdom, purple is a wonderful choice. Use your instincts and see what feels correct to you.

When you are done coloring and setting the eggs out to dry, repeat the following incantation:

At this magickal time of year,
Wishes are heard both loud and clear.
With these eggs it's my intent
To use them as an implement
That carries my wishes to the destination
Where requests are honored without hesitation.
So Mote It Be

When you're ready to dispose of your eggs, save the shells and grind them into powder. You can use that to protect your home by sprinkling it around the border of your property.

Energizing Eggshell Powder

Eggshells may be fragile when you bump them or drop them, but when you grind them into powder, they are a very strong ally when creating magick. Believed to possess a purifying energy, eggshell powder—also known as cascarilla powder—can be used to cast circles, sprinkled over doorways and other thresholds for protection, and even used to make magickal candles around Ostara/Easter. The candles can be used for spells for protection, healing, resurrection, and fertility. Keep a jar of eggshell powder in your cupboard as a staple. You never know when it will come in handy.

You will need:

· Eggshells

· A mortar and pestle

· A jar with a tight-fitting lid

After you eat the eggs, wash and dry the eggshells and set them aside until you have a few to work with. Once the shells are totally dry, check to see if there is a thin membrane on the inner eggshell. If so, this must be removed before grinding the shells.

Grind the eggshells into a powder, put the powder into the jar, then hold the jar in your hands. Repeat the following incantation to charge the powder.

Ostara—March 19–22

I energize this power to help me along,
With doing my bidding and keeping me strong.
So Mote It Be

Then send your energy down from your arms into your hands and from your hands into the jar.

Butterfly Wish

Butterflies are one of the ultimate symbols of spring. Let the gossamer wings of a butterfly carry your wishes far and wide, so that they may manifest and return to you. A Native American legend states that to make a heart's wish come true, you must capture a butterfly without harming it, hold it in your cupped palms, and whisper your wish to it. Release the butterfly and let it fly away. This spell recreates the magick while removing any chance of accidentally harming a living butterfly. You will need:

- A picture of a butterfly or butterfly amulet

Hold the picture or amulet cupped in your hands as though you were cradling a real butterfly and repeat the following incantation:

I have a wish that's important to me,
And I trust in your ability to oversee.
Please take my wish up in the sky,
Farther than I can see with my eye.
Go to the place where wishes come true,
The place that's known only by you.
And with your delivery, I do pray,
My wish will be granted this very day.
So Mote It Be

Whisper your wish to the butterfly and put it away in a safe place until your wish is granted. You can repeat the incantation as often is necessary. You can even make a small paper airplane covered in butterfly colors and toss it to the winds.

Holy Week Manifestation

Two of the holiest celebrations of the year begin this week with Easter and Passover. Those two holidays have more in common than you might think because both are celebrations of rebirth. Christians will be celebrating the resurrection of Jesus while Jews will celebrate the liberation of the Israelites and their return to their ancestral land. You don't have to be religious to be reborn. Holy Week is a good time to resurrect yourself and your life, and fulfill your inner desires.

You will need:

- Bay leaves
- A pen
- A heatproof bowl or cauldron

Write each of your wishes on a separate leaf, and with each leaf, focus on your intent. When you're done, go outside and burn the leaves to release that energy into the universe. As the leaves start to burn, repeat the following incantation:

Sacred smoke, send my wishes high.
My life I need to modify.
With bay leaves and fire, all I require
Is that you grant me these essential desires.
So Mote It Be

Watch the smoke rise as the leaves burn and if your intent was honest and strong, you will be given good results.

Job Interview Spell

Ostara is the season for new beginnings. Are you nervous about doing well in an upcoming job interview? Use the following candle spell to bolster your confidence and present yourself in a positive way.

You will need:

Ostara—March 19–22

- A yellow candle

- A topaz stone

The night before the interview, sit down, light the candle, take a few cleansing breaths, and meditate for five minutes to send out positive energy. Then hold the topaz in your hand and repeat this incantation:

I know this is the job for me.
Let them see it and agree.
I am the perfect candidate.
A positive outcome I await.
So Mote It Be

Put the stone down, blow out the candle, and rub the smoke between your palms, then open your hands, palms up, and release your intentions into the ether.

Whether you're going to the interview in person or doing it virtually, wear or carry the stone with you.

Mother Earth Protection Spell

I think many of us are on edge and worrying about what might happen next in this crazy, unpredictable world. Here is a spell to protect those who are under attack as well as protect the world itself.

You will need:

- A purple and a white candle

- Frankincense

- Clear quartz

- A piece of paper with your message (written in black ink) to the universe about regaining peace and harmony

Put the candles on top of your message, then light the candles and the incense.

Take the quartz crystal in your hand and repeat the following incantation:

Protect the world from violence and pain.
Protect it from those who are filled with disdain.
Protect us from anger, hardship, and greed.
Protect us from those who lie and mislead.
Stop the insanity and hear my plea.
This is my wish.
So Mote It Be

Plant an Egg Abundance Spell

Eggs have been associated with creation, new life, and rebirth for as long as humans have recorded history. This spell, however, is designed to bring you prosperity, whether it be financial or otherwise.

You will need:

· A marker

· A raw, uncooked egg still in its unbroken shell

· A packet of seeds of your choice

Take the marker and write what you are asking for on the egg. Bury the egg in a pot, either indoors or out, depending on what you're planting, then repeat the following incantation:

Egg for nourishment and for growth,
Wish for abundance and this is my oath:
When the seedlings start to grow,
And their leaves begin to show,
Nurture them with loving care,
And also offer them a prayer.
As the plant makes its breakthrough,
Your abundance will come to you.
So Mote It Be

When you first plant the seeds, and as you see the plant grow, thank the plant spirits for their help as well.

Ostara—March 19–22

Plant Your Crystals

When it comes to raising vibrations and boosting your garden, crystals are holistic healers, and when you put the healing powers of gemstones and gardening together, your garden will flourish. Whether you have your plants in pots or in the ground, indoors or out, a crystal boost can make all the difference in the world.

All crystals have different properties and characteristics. To choose the best crystal for your plants, you have to look to the energies they provide.

You will need any crystal of your choice.

Some people might use only one clear quartz for the entire garden, but depending on your need for a specific plant, you can add crystals whenever needed.

Make sure your crystals are cleansed. You can do this with incense smoke, leaving them out under a full moon, or using the protective white light where you hold the crystal in your hands and visualize a bright white light filling the crystal.

Right before using the crystals, hold them in your hands and repeat the following incantation:

Precious crystals shining bright,
Support my garden day and night.
Keep it healthy and free from pests,
And manifest its level best.
So Mote It Be

You can either place the crystals at the base of the plant when you repot it or dig a shallow hole in the dirt so it can make direct contact with the plant's roots. Some choose to hang crystals all around the garden instead, and placing gnomes—the elemental spirits of earth energy—can offer support and protection as well. No matter what you decide, your honest intentions will make your garden thrive.

Spring Cleaning

When spring arrives, it's time to get rid of the residue from winter and clean your house. Not only will you be getting rid of dust and dirt, but you will also be clearing from your space any bad vibes that may be lingering in the dust. It's time to get rid of the old to make room for the new, not just physically, but energetically, too.

You will need:

- Your usual cleaning supplies

- An herb bundle, stick of palo santo, or incense—cinnamon, nag champa, rose, frankincense, copal, jasmine, sandalwood, or dragon's blood

Get started on a bright sunny day. Open all your windows because fresh air is cleansing, and it gets the energy moving. If the air in your home is stagnant, that will affect how you feel.

While you are cleaning, focus your intention on attracting harmony, prosperity, protection, and health to your home.

Make sure you wipe down your doorframes and windowsills to block negative energy from getting in, and wash the outside of your front and back doors, too. Don't forget to wash the windows, because once they are clean, positive energy can come through. Work from the top down.

Before you begin your usual cleaning routine, repeat the following incantation:

> With vacuum, mop, and dust rag, I now begin my chore
> Of sweeping negativity right out of the door.
> Fresh air and hard scrubbing will make this house glow
> And allow the good energy to flourish and flow.
> May the troubles of winter be out of the way,
> And this house will be peaceful and safe night and day.
> So Mote It Be

Spring cleaning usually takes more than one day, so repeat this incantation each time you resume cleaning. At the end of each day, light the sage,

Ostara—March 19–22

palo santo, or incense and walk through each room to clear and unblock the atmosphere.

A Thousand Wishes

This shower spell is the opposite of the spells that wash negativity away. Instead, it draws in positivity. It came to mind when I tried a new body wash called A Thousand Wishes and it got me thinking that if we can wash away negativity as we bathe, we can also make wishes by using soap with the fragrances we use for manifesting.

You will need:

- A jasmine, lavender, vanilla, patchouli, sandalwood, white sage, or rose soap or body wash

As you lather up, speak the wishes you are asking for aloud and visualize in your mind the wish coming true. Don't worry about washing your wishes down the drain when you rinse. These floral fragrances stick to you long after you rinse and dry off. When you're done, recite the following incantation:

These wishes were asked for because there's a need.
I send them with love and not out of greed.
And since I am the wish creator,
I ask that they come through sooner than later.
So Mote It Be

Alternatively, you can make your own magickal body wash. This is a simple, natural body wash that takes only minutes to prepare. Remember to use only skin-safe essential oils, and always patch test any essential oils you use on the inside of your arm forty-eight hours before using them in your body wash. Also remember that it's best not to use plastic bottles for body washes containing essential oils. If you can, opt for a glass bottle with a pump for easy dispensing, and keep it out of direct sunlight.

You will need:

- ⅓ cup liquid castile soap

- ⅓ cup raw honey

- ⅓ cup carrier oil such as olive oil, jojoba oil, or fractionated coconut oil

- 10 drops jasmine, lavender, patchouli, rose, or sandalwood oil—or use a combination!

Mix all ingredients together in a glass measuring cup and then pour into your glass pump bottle. Use while bathing or showering, while thinking about your intention. It's as simple as that.

To Find What's Lost

While he has other attributes as well, Hermes is the god of lost and found so if you have misplaced anything, ask Hermes for help. You will need to make an offering. Here are some of the things that you can use: frankincense; lavender or strawberry incense; coins; feathers; amethyst, alexandrite, or smoky quartz gemstones; honey, wine, or milk.

April is a great month to do this spell, since the number four is sacred to Hermes, as he was born in the fourth month. For an extra boost, do this spell on a Wednesday, which is Hermes's sacred day.

You will need:

- A red candle

- Pen and paper

Gather your offerings and then write the object that you wish to find in blue ink on the paper. Then light the candle and repeat the following incantation:

> Hermes, god of lost and found,
> I need you now to be around
> To help retrieve what I must find,
> Because it's left me in a bind.
> Please grant me the keen perception,
> To send me in the right direction.
> Then open my eyes and let me see
> The object that eluded me.
> So Mote It Be

Ostara—March 19–22

Soon you should get an idea of where the lost item is.

Repeat the spell if needed.

Healing Candle Spell

This very easy spell works wonders because whether it is you that needs healing or you're doing this for someone else, your strong intent will bring it to fruition.

You will need:

• A blue candle

As you light the candle, focus on the area that needs healing, and then recite this incantation:

Magick candle, [name] needs your healing.
Take away that harmful feeling.
Illness begone is what I require.
A clean bill of health must now transpire.
So Mote It Be

Blow out the candle when you're done and repeat this spell as often as necessary.

New Pet Blessing

National Pet Adoption Day is April 30th. It's always a blessing when a new pet enters our lives. Here is a blessing for the new member of the family.

You will need:

• A photo or drawing of your new pet

• A blue candle

• Rose or gardenia incense or oil

• A rose quartz crystal

• A small velvet pouch

- A simple gold ring or hoop
- A sprig of fresh marjoram or sprinkle of the dry herb

Place the candle next to the picture, light the incense or anoint the candle with the oil, then take the rose quartz crystal in your hand and say:

> With an open heart and unconditional love, I welcome you into my life.

Then pick up the gold ring and say:

> This ring symbolizes eternity. May our souls never be parted.

With the crystal and ring in your hand say:

> You are my child and I promise you love and protection forever and always.
> So Mote It Be

Blow out the candle, place the crystal and ring in the pouch along with the sprig of marjoram, and put it in a safe place where it will not be disturbed.

Moon Water

Some people consider Moon Water a variation of holy water, and in some ways, it is.

Moon Water is a water-based lunar potion that is created during a chosen moon phase. It is usually collected during the full moon when the moon's energy is said to be at its fullest, but depending on the intended use of Moon Water, all lunar phases will work. In my opinion, the only time you should not make Moon Water is during an eclipse because eclipse energy overpowers lunar energy.

There are many uses for Moon Water. It can be used to transform situations, enhance psychic abilities, amplify magickal power, trigger inspiration, encourage love, offer tranquility, and more. It is also used for spiritual healing, watering plants, bathing and cleaning, blessing, rituals, charging, or anything else that involves the moon.

Ostara—March 19–22

You can make what I call an all-purpose jar to be used for many reasons, but you can also make many kinds of different jars to manifest different intentions.

You will need:

- A clean glass jar
- Water
- Full moon or the lunar phase of your choice
- Optional: crystals that won't dissolve
- Optional: herbs

Moon Water is easy to concoct.

Get a clean glass jar, and fill it with distilled, spring, tap, or purified water. Set the jar under a full moon and leave it out overnight. Make sure it's not in contact with sunlight because that will change its properties.

You can also add water-safe crystals like clear quartz, rose quartz, or amethyst, or herbs like mugwort, which is ruled by the moon and good for cleansing. Lavender is used for calming, and for protection, use rosemary. Charms, amulets, or talismans can be used as well.

I was taught not to keep Moon Water longer than about a month, unless it's fresh, natural spring water, which is supposed to last sixty days or so, because water can grow bacteria and stagnate. Others believe that if the water is kept clean and refrigerated in a sealed container, it can last for several months or even up to a year. Moon Water with herbs should be stored in a cool, dark place.

Moon Phase Meanings

New moons bring new beginnings and a clean slate.

The waxing crescent moon sets intentions and fresh energy. Send out your hopes and desires.

The first-quarter moon means challenges. It's time to take action.

The waxing gibbous moon is all about having patience. Sit back and observe.

The full moon is all about harvesting endeavors, times to gather your intentions, peak energy, and blessings.

The waning gibbous moon is about being introspective. Look within, release, and receive.

The third-quarter moon is about release and letting go, transition, and adjustment.

The waning crescent moon means surrender. It's time for rest and recuperation.

The new moon again means new beginnings, rest, and restoration.

Ostara Recipes

Magickal Properties of Herbs and Botanicals

For Courage: Pepper, basil, chives, and horseradish

For Health: Allspice, cinnamon, garlic, coriander, poppy seed, and chamomile

For Love: Coriander, vanilla, and cinnamon

For Luck: Allspice, nutmeg, and heather

For Money: Dill, basil, ginger, bay leaves, cinnamon, and spearmint

For Peace: Marjoram, mint, sage, and lemon balm

For Protection: Salt, marjoram, basil, bay, cinnamon, garlic, peppermint, and pepper

For Psychic Awareness: Star anise, lemongrass, and sage

For Success: Bay, rosemary, saffron, and marjoram

Ostara—March 19–22

For Wisdom: Bay leaves, basil, chamomile, dill, marjoram, parsley, thyme, cumin, and sage

Magickal Properties of Fruit in Cooking

Apple: Love, health, and longevity

Banana: Fertility and strength

Blackberry: Prosperity, protection, and abundance

Blueberry: Tranquility, peace, protection, and prosperity

Cherry: Passion and love

Coconut: Fertility and chastity

Dragon Fruit: Creativity and sexuality

Grapes: Prosperity and fertility

Kiwi: Fertility and love

Lemon: Purification, protection, and health

Lime: Happiness, purification, and healing

Mango: Spirituality and happiness

Orange: Joy, health, and purification

Peach: Spirituality, fertility, love, and harmony

Pear: Love, health, and prosperity

Pineapple: Prosperity, love, and friendship

Pomegranate: Wish-granting and ancestor work

Raspberry: Love and protection

Strawberry: Love, peace, happiness, luck, and aphrodisiac

Watermelon: Fertility, prosperity, good health, and joy

Dilly Pink Pickled Eggs

Pink pickled eggs for Ostara? Of course!

½ cup beet juice
1 cup water
1 teaspoon salt
1 teaspoon whole peppercorns
2 cloves garlic, smashed
2 teaspoons pickling spice
12 hard-boiled eggs, peeled

Combine all the ingredients except the eggs in a saucepan and bring it to a boil, then lower the heat and let it simmer for fifteen minutes. Let it cool.

Place eggs in a four-cup glass jar with a lid, then pour the juice over the eggs. Cover the jar and place it in the refrigerator. Let them marinate for three to four days before serving.

Prefer another spring color? Feel free to get creative! You could use turmeric powder for bright orange-yellow eggs or butterfly pea flower tea to dye the eggs a vibrant blue. Nature is full of all kinds of wonderful natural dyes; let spring guide your hand.

PART V

Beltane—May 1

Also referred to as May Day, Beltane is a Celtic fire festival, literally meaning "bright fire" and referring to ritual extinguishing and rekindling of all fires. Fire means warmth, life, and transformation. The sun god comes to the earth goddess signaling good fortune and change. It is celebrated with bonfires, maypoles, and dancing. The Celts honored the fertility of the gods with gifts and offerings. Cattle were driven through the smoke of the balefires and blessed with health and fertility for the coming year. The Hill of Tara is a sacred and ancient ceremonial and burial site located in County Meath, Ireland. There, the fires of Tara were the first ones lit every year at Beltane. All other fires were then lit with a flame from Tara.

Beltane is the first day of summer according to the Wheel and celebrates the half of the year dedicated to growth and fertility. This is a celebration of life above all!

Symbols: The maypole, flower wreaths, and cows adorned with flowers

Activities: As Beltane is the great wedding of the goddess and the god, it is a popular time for Pagan weddings or handfastings, dressing trees with colorful ribbons, lighting bonfires, and dancing around the maypole. Decorate homes, barns, and other buildings with green budding branches, make and wear garland wreaths of flowers and greens, and welcome the fae into your life, garden, and home.

Incense: Frankincense, lilac, passionflower, rose, vanilla, patchouli, and dragon's blood

Spell Work: Protection, cleansing, and fertility magick

Deities: Belenus, Flora, Artemis, Cernunnos, Hera, Pan, and Aphrodite

Gemstones: Sapphire, bloodstone, emerald, orange carnelian, and rose quartz

Trees, Fruits, and Herbs: Mint, marjoram, rosemary, mugwort, cherries, and assorted berries

Animal: Honeybee, cat, frog, goat, rabbit, and swallow

Colors: Green, red, yellow, blue, pink, and white

Elementals

The Swiss alchemist, Paracelsus, one of the forefathers of modern medicine, classified elemental beings in accordance with each element of earth. According to folklore, there are four groups of elementals. Each possesses energies that embody its element. They are an enduring part of many ritual forms, especially in modern witchcraft.

Gnomes—Earth

Gnomes are elemental nature spirits that tend the earth through the cycles of the four seasons and see to it that all living things are supplied with their daily needs. They also process the waste and by-products that are an inevitable part of our everyday existence, purginig the earth of poisons and pollutants that are dangerous to the physical bodies of human, animal, and plant life. On a metaphysical level, it's a gnome's task to do away with the fallout of mankind's unrest, hostility, and negativity, which affects the energetic levels in the earth.

Undines—Water
Undines are guardians of the gardens of the seas. They are beautiful mermaid-like beings who can change form rapidly. They can control the tides and have much to do with the climate as well as oxygenation and precipitation. They work ceaselessly to heal the polluted seas while recharging the electromagnetic field of the waters.

Sylphs—Air
These air spirits reside in the skies. They act out the will and spirit of the air. With sacred breath, they tend the air element, direct the flow of air currents and atmospheric conditions, and purify the atmosphere. Their supernatural power is shape-shifting into cloud shapes and forms of light, flight, and invisibility.

Salamanders—Fire
These small, lizard-sized creatures live within the etheric force of fire. It is said that they are invulnerable to fire, are born to the flames, and rule the element of fire. They are the strongest and most powerful of all the elementals, having the ability to extend or diminish their size as needed. They and others of their kind are mischievous spirits.

Never Step into a Faerie Ring

A great deal of folklore exists about fairy rings, but before you can heed the warning, you need to know what a fairy ring is.

In the mundane world, a fairy ring—which is also referred to as a fairy circle, elf circle, elf ring, or pixie ring—is a naturally occurring ring of mushrooms. The rings may grow quite large in diameter, and they become stable over time as the fungus grows and seeks food underground. They are found mainly in forested areas, but also appear in grasslands or rangelands. They are the subject of much folklore and myth worldwide, particularly in western Europe. They are often seen as hazardous or dangerous places.

Beltane—May 1

Fairy rings are worn areas in the grass made, according to folklore, by fairies dancing. It is believed that they are where fairies came to celebrate and perform many of the rituals of their own magick. The mushrooms were used as stools for the fairies to rest up a bit during the evening's festivities. It is believed that those who join the fairy dance within the circle under the moon are sometimes lost to time and place, and may even disappear forever.

There are many stories written on fairy history, folklore, and superstitions, from many different cultures.

In German folklore, it is believed that these rings mark the place where witches gather and dance. The term for them in German is *hexenringe*, or "witches' rings." Old Dutch superstitions state that the rings are where the devil churns his milk. Austria has a legend that the rings are created by dragons. Similar tales arise in French and Scandinavian folklore, and stories of tiny spirits inhabiting these rings come from the Philippines as well.

Most of the stories talk about the terrible consequences of interfering in the lives of fairies, like revealing their location, stepping into their ring, or trying to capture them. Sometimes just running into a fairy by chance can change a person's life. Take, for instance, the tale of Thomas the Rhymer, the 13th-century bard who reputedly vanished for seven years. When he finally returned, he possessed the gift of prophecy— something that he had not previously had. In accordance, he was given the name "True Thomas." But where was Thomas for those seven years? According to him, he had been in Fairyland.

But Thomas isn't the only soul who has been swept away to the realm of fairy. Most often, if someone is enticed to enter a fairy ring and dance with the fairies for at least twenty minutes, they will find upon leaving the ring that many years in the third dimension have passed.

An Irish folktale tells of a girl who was returning home with bread when she heard music. Curious, she went to see where it was coming from and encountered a group of fairies having a jolly time. They beckoned her to dance with them and she stepped inside the fairy ring. She danced for a while, then told them she must go home because her mother was waiting for her. When she entered her house, she was shocked to see

114 *Magick for All Seasons*

that her mother was twenty years older. When her mother asked where she had been, the girl said she only went to the market to buy bread, and then handed her that fresh loaf of bread. The child didn't age, but twenty years had passed on earth.

So, if you were walking alone in the woods and heard music and saw fairies dancing inside the ring, would you enter? Or would you, perhaps, try to snap a photograph?

Beltane Spells
Beltane/May Day Magickal Wishing Tree

Historically, Beltane celebrations included decorating trees and bushes with brightly colored strips of ribbon or fabric. These would be hung from branches and entwined into greenery to serve as an offering to the fairies that live in and around the plants. Adorning their homes demonstrated respect, affection, and veneration and was believed to be a way to encourage the fairies to grant your wishes, should they be feeling generous. Today, this tradition is less widely practiced, but if you see colorful ribbons hanging from plants, you'll know why. This ritual is easy to recreate. You will need:

- Colored ribbons, strips of cloth, or paper

- A pen or marker

- A tree or bush

Write your wish or wishes on the ribbons, cloth, or paper and hang them on your tree or bush. If you're living somewhere without trees or bushes, tie the ribbons to hangers in a window, in the path of a fan or air conditioner, off a balcony, to a fence or gate, or anywhere the wind blows or there are breezes. Repeat the following incantation:

> With these ribbons it's my intent
> To celebrate this sabbat event.
> May nature inspire me,
> May love surround me,

Beltane—May 1

May spirit protect me, and
May my wishes come true.
So Mote It Be.

Making a May Basket

The tradition of May baskets dates back to German Pagan rituals from the 12th and 13th centuries. They say that May baskets are a forgotten tradition, but everything old can become new again, and delivering a basket can brighten the day of someone who is lucky enough to find one on their doorstep. The publication *The Old Farmer's Almanac* reports that this was a popular custom in the 19th and 20th centuries. People would fill a paper cone or a basket with treats and flowers. Then they would knock on the recipient's door and yell, "May basket!" and run away. If they got caught, the gifter would owe the giftee a kiss.

You will need:

- A basket or other container

- Flowers or other ethically gathered greenery

- Sweet treats like cookies or candy

- Your imagination!

Baskets come in all shapes and sizes and can be made of bags, boxes, or actual woven baskets. They are usually filled with flowers and other greenery from the yard and treats like baked goods and candy. Use your imagination and put in anything the giftee would enjoy.

Garden Spirits Blessing with Sun Water

During spring and summer, we are outside among nature and many of us are tending our gardens. It makes good sense to call upon the garden spirits to ensure the health of our plants and consecrate the plants with Sun Water, which is often used in spells and rituals for protection, healing, and cleansing.

You will need:

- A clear glass jar with a lid—the size of your outdoor or indoor garden will determine the size of the jar you need to use
- Water to fill the jar
- A quartz crystal

Place the crystal in the jar and fill it with water. Close the lid, take the jar in both hands, and set your intentions. Concentrate on keeping your plants healthy and thriving whether they be your garden or indoor plants.

Once the intention is set, place the jar outside in the sun or on a sunny windowsill and let the water charge for at least four hours. Just make sure you bring it inside before sunset because if you leave it out all night, the moon's energy will affect it.

When you're ready to call upon the plant spirits and bless your plants, the easiest way is to put the water in a spray bottle and give each plant a spritz while you repeat this incantation:

I call upon all plant spirits to help my garden grow.
Keep it healthy and robust and keep it all aglow.
Nurture and protect them from things that can impair.
I know that with your best intent you'll give it loving care.
So Mote It Be

When you're done, thank the plant spirits for their assistance, and you can leave them an offering of things like honey, milk, seeds, nuts, berries, vegetables, and fruits of the season.

Grounding Spell

Grounding, also known as earthing, is the process of connecting to the earth's electrical energy. This practice relies on earthing science and grounding physics to explain how the electrical charges from the earth have positive effects on your body, such as reducing inflammation, pain, and stress. It also improves blood flow energy and a feeling of greater well-being.

You will need:

- Nothing but yourself

There are many ways to do a grounding. The easiest way is to walk barefoot, but some prefer to sit or lie on the ground instead.

When you are ready, repeat this incantation:

I'm sending my roots deep into the ground,
The results of which will be profound.
Heal what needs healing the natural way.
Send illness and bad vibes far and away.
So Mote It Be

Knot Your Troubles Away

It would be nice if we could be trouble-free but the second-best thing to do is take your troubles, bind them in knots, and get rid of them.

You will need:

- A piece of colored yarn, about twelve inches long. The color should correspond with the problem: green for money and financial issues, red for love dilemmas, purple for psychic blocks, and so forth.

Hold one end of the yarn in each hand, concentrate on your problem, and start tying knots in the yarn. Visualize all your troubles getting bound up in the knots and trapped. Keep tying until you feel it's enough. When you're done knotting, take the knots outside and bury them, then recite this incantation:

Knots will bind my problems tight,
And they'll be made with all my might.
This issue will now go away,
Starting from this very day.
The knots will be tossed into a hole,
And begone forever.
That is my goal.
So Mote It Be

118   *Magick for All Seasons*

White Light Protection Spell

They say that white light is the space within the universe that stores positive energies and can be used in many ways. Call upon the white light when you feel the need for protection from harm of any kind. The power of the white light is infinite and can be used on yourself, someone else, your pets, your home, your belongings, or the whole of Mother Earth.

You will need:

- A quiet place to sit
- A white candle

Light the candle, close your eyes, and in your mind's eye, see what you are asking protection from. Concentrate on your goal and envision a tiny spot of bright white light manifesting itself. Watch it spread bigger and bigger until it surrounds the person, place, or thing that needs protection. Once you see that happening, recite the following incantation:

> White light, shining bright, I ask for your protection.
> All harm will be repelled by your bright reflection.
> Keep your energy pure and strong
> To do its job to right the wrong.
> So Mote It Be

Once the spell is in place, you can blow out the candle or let it burn itself out. Sometimes with candle spells, I use flameless battery-operated candles to avoid a fire hazard, and so they can remain on indefinitely.

The Warning Spell

If you feel like someone is intimidating you in any way, you can cast this spell to let them know that you will fight back if they don't cease. But before you decide to act, send out this warning.

You will need:

- A black candle

Light the candle and repeat the name of the person who you think will do you harm. Then recite this incantation:

Beltane—May 1

If I feel harmed in any way,
I promise there will be Hell to pay.
If you really force me to,
I'll have to give it back to you.
An eye for an eye and tooth for a tooth,
You will face the moment of truth.
So now think twice before you proceed,
Or pay the price for your dastardly deed.
You'll get it back in three times three,
I promise you that.
So Mote It Be.

Blow out the candle and watch as the smoke rises up into the universe, carrying your message to the person that needs to be forewarned.

Toss the ashes into the air and let the breeze carry them away.

Return to Your Source

You can't have too many ways of getting rid of anything dark and evil that comes your way. You have the power to send it back. All it takes is your intentions and a quick spell.

You will need:

- A black candle

- Patchouli, sandalwood, or myrrh essential oil

Anoint the candle with the essential oil then light the candle and repeat the following incantation:

Turn around, go back to your source, you're not welcome here.
This environment will never accept that kind of atmosphere.
The person that chose to send you this way
Will very soon have some karma to pay.
So Mote It Be

Blow out the candle and repeat this spell as often as you need to.

Stir Up Some Happiness

This is probably going to be one of the simplest spells you will ever do, but don't let the simplicity fool you.

You will need:

- A cup of coffee, tea, or any other favorite beverage that can be stirred
- A spoon or a coffee stirrer

Sit down with your drink, begin to stir it in a clockwise direction, and repeat the following incantation:

> Sadness and trouble, I keep you at bay.
> Stirring up happiness will come my way.
> So Mote It Be

Stir as long as you wish and, as you stir, visualize happiness filling your cup. Drink deep from your own personal well of joy. (Just make sure it's cool enough first!)

May a little bit of magick float into your life today.

Pet Protection Bell

Bells have a number of uses. They call people to prayer, announce a victory, and alert people of impending danger. Historically, the sound of ringing church bells was believed to banish demons and other malevolent entities. Some people place a bell on their cat's collar to give birds and small animals a heads up that danger is nearby, but a bell on a pet's collar can keep them from harm as well.

You will need:

- A pet collar with a bell. (I suggest one that is designed to break away if the collar gets caught on something.)

Before you put the collar on your pet, hold it in your hands and recite the following incantation:

May this bell keep danger away,
And safeguard (name of the pet) both night and day.
The sound of the bell will work as a shield,
To force negativity to instantly yield.
So Mote It Be

If you can't find a collar with a bell, you can get a small jingle bell and sew it onto the collar, but make sure you sew it on tight (but also not too tight) to avoid a choking hazard.

Seven-Day Memorial Altar Spell

Many people have friends or loved ones both past and present who have enlisted in the armed forces. When Veteran's Day and Memorial Day come to pass, create an altar to pay homage to the men and women who have served our nation in a variety of ways. An altar can be large and elaborate or as tiny as a single candle. You can put it on a tabletop, the top shelf of a bookcase, or small nook somewhere in the house that won't be disturbed. Keep the light shining for the next seven days in their honor.

You will need:

- A white candle

- A photo of those whom you want to remember

- A personal belonging of that person or persons

If you do not have any photos or personal belongings, you can simply write their names on a piece of paper and put a picture of an American flag or a symbol of whichever branch of the armed forces they belonged to.

Place the photos or belongings around the candle, then light the candle and repeat the following incantation:

This altar is created in respect,
And gives me the chance to recollect
On your strength and courage in times of strife,
And keeping us free in our daily life.
For seven days this light will glow,
And that's because I want you to know
You're in my thoughts eternally,
And there you shall stay.
So Mote It Be

Saint Anthony Spell: Tony, Tony

When you need to find something, turn to Saint Anthony. All you need to do is repeat the following:

Tony, Tony, look around!
Help me find what must be found.

Happy Aquarium Spell

Clean Your Aquarium Day is on June 18th, promoting a reminder to everyone who owns a fish tank to clean it regularly and keep their fish healthy and happy. Fish are people, too. I used to have a nice saltwater aquarium and had all sorts of interesting creatures. From time to time, other animals shared the tank with the fish, like hermit crabs, porcelain crabs, anemones, branded coral shrimps, and even tiny eels. For those of you who have aquariums or even goldfish in a bowl, here's a spell to help them thrive. This spell can be cast while you're setting up a new tank or on an existing tank.

You will need:

- A Pisces or Aquarius amulet or talisman

- The deity of your choice (If you have a saltwater aquarium, you might want to call upon Aphrodite, Amphitrite, or Poseidon. For freshwater, call upon Egeria or Tethys.)

Beltane—May 1

Place the amulet next to the tank, call upon the deity that you have chosen to watch over your tank, and dedicate it to them by saying:

[Name of deity],
I dedicate this tank in your honor.
Please make it a healthy environment for all the lovely creatures living within.
Watch over them and keep them safe from harm.
So Mote It Be

Repeat the incantation whenever you change the tank water or add new creatures to the tank.

Sachet of Protection

Sachets are made for many reasons. Some just make one up because the scent is wonderful, or they can be made for a specific intention. With this protection sachet, you get both. Not only will you get the protection you want, but also a wonderful scent as well.

You will need:

- A small cloth bag with a drawstring or small bowl

- A clear quartz crystal

- A combination of any of these protective ingredients: rosemary, peppermint, bay leaf, lemon peel, cinnamon sticks, myrrh, patchouli, jasmine, mint, basil, lavender, eucalyptus, orange peel, sage, sandalwood, cloves, amber, or palo santo

Place the ingredients into the sachet bag and tie it shut. If you don't have a sachet bag, you can put the ingredients into a bowl. Hold the bag or bowl in your hands, and send energy into the ingredients and say, "Keep this place safe. So Mote It Be."

Hang the bag or place the bowl in a safe place where it won't be disturbed and replenish it when the scent starts to fade.

Here are some other ingredients used for specific purposes:

For Creativity: Clove, ginger, hyssop, and verbena

For Drawing Money: Bay leaf, basil, cinnamon, frankincense, and orange

For Empowerment: Jasmine, bay leaf, rosemary, orange, sage, and cinnamon

For Removing Negative Energies: Bay leaf, cinnamon, dried lemon slice, and myrrh

For Success: Allspice, cinnamon, frankincense, myrrh, patchouli, vanilla, jasmine, and ginger

Witch Bottle of Protection

The witch's bottle of protection does what it says. This is a very old spell device. It serves as a trap for negative energy that may be directed at you. These bottles will keep the negativity at bay.

The traditional witch's bottle is a small flask of blue or green glass, about three inches high, but modern practitioners often use small glass jars with tight-fitting lids instead.

To make a simple witch's bottle, fill a glass jar halfway with sharp objects such as pins, broken glass, or old razor blades. Then throw in a few sprigs of rosemary and fill the jar with red wine. Way back when, the bottles contained urine, hair, nail clippings, or menstrual blood, but while some diehard practitioners still do that today, in recent years, the witch bottles have taken on a gentler tone.

After your bottle is filled, seal it tightly with candle wax and it's time to do an incantation to get the protective forces moving.

The incantation I use most often is:

Sharper than a serpent's tongue, these objects do my bidding.
To attract all negative energy and assist me with the ridding
Of jealousy and spite and greed and all things negative sent.
Trap them here inside the glass before they start to vent.
So Mote It Be

Beltane—May 1

Beltane Recipes

Bannocks

Bannocks are a traditional Celtic bread. Originally made from unleavened barley or oatmeal dough, modern bannocks can be made with a variety of flours. (Oats are especially plentiful at Beltane.) Folklore says that bannocks are a favorite food of household faeries and the Scottish brownie.

> 3 cups flour
> 1 cup water
> 2 teaspoons baking powder
> ½ teaspoon salt
> 4 tablespoons vegetable oil, plus 1 tablespoon
> ½ teaspoon sugar
> dried fruit, chopped
> nuts, seeds

Mix your dry ingredients in a large mixing bowl, then add four tablespoons of vegetable oil. Pour in the water until a smooth consistency is achieved.

Bring the dough together with your hands. Remove it from the bowl then lightly knead the dough on a floured surface. Don't do too much. Ten kneads will do.

Line your pot or frying pan with parchment paper and douse with the remaining oil. Heat on medium to low heat.

Pop your dough into the pot or skillet. Cook until golden brown, about ten to fifteen minutes on each side. Pierce the bannock with a skewer to see if it's ready. When the dough no longer sticks to the skewer, it's done.

Smear butter on the finished quick bread if you like, and there you have it.

Super Moon Refreshment

When the moon is bright and full, here is a soothing sipper for your super moon watching. This recipe is so simple, and friends swear by its gentle and ethereal effectiveness to heal and calm.

a pitcher
paper towels
rolling pin (or any kitchen hoo-ha to crush the leaves)
optional: clean, clear quartz crystal
spring water
about ½ cup fresh mint (either homegrown or store bought
   is fine)

Get out your pitcher. Clear glass is best if you intend to take the last step and incorporate the quartz crystal, but any clean pitcher will do.

Fill the pitcher about three-quarters of the way full of spring water. Set it aside.

Cut about half a cup of mint sprigs from your stash or buy mint (only fresh, never dried) from the store. If your pitcher is on the larger side, you'll need more. Use your own judgment; some people like it mintier than others.

Place the mint between two paper towels and *gently* crush with a rolling pin until the aroma of the mint is stronger. Gently stir into the pitcher of spring water. Let the leaves filter through the water.

If this is all you need, then refrigerate for a few hours and let the mint infuse the water.

If you want a little extra magickal boost, however, you can also add a clear, clean quartz crystal to your mint water. Adding nontoxic gemstones to water is an ancient practice. It can't hurt (as long as you check to make sure the gems you use are nontoxic and safe to submerge in water) and might help. So if you'd like to incorporate this practice into your mint water, place a clean quartz crystal in the bottom of the pitcher before you add the spring water. Be sure to remove the crystal before drinking.

Beltane—May 1

For a more potent drink for later, make a separate pitcher with your quartz crystal included and leave it out all night under the supermoon. You might be pleasantly surprised.

Sorcerous Lentil Salad

This salad would bring a smile to the face of even of the wickedest of witches. Use green or black lentils; red lentils will dissolve easily when boiled.

1½ cups lentils
½ teaspoon salt
½ cup chopped parsley
6 green onions, chopped
8 tablespoons olive oil
juice of 2 lemons
2 cloves garlic, crushed
black pepper to taste
¼ teaspoon ground coriander
¼ teaspoon ground cumin

Soak the lentils in ample water for a few hours.

Bring them to a boil and simmer until tender, but not mushy, about thirty minutes. Drain and cool them.

Place the lentils in a salad bowl and add salt, parsley, and green onions. Mix the olive oil, lemon juice, garlic, black pepper, coriander, and cumin. Toss with the lentils and chill.

Serves six.

Spellbound Sugar Cookies

After a busy day of stirring the cauldron, a sweet treat is in order. And when you take these easy-to-make cookies out of the oven, they will put a spell on you.

1½ cups powdered sugar
1 cup butter
1 egg

1½ teaspoons vanilla
1 teaspoon baking soda
1 teaspoon cream tartar
granulated sugar to taste

Mix all the ingredients together then refrigerate the cookie dough for three hours.

Divide the dough in half and roll it thin, around a quarter of an inch thick.

Get out your favorite cookie cutters, cut the cookies, then sprinkle with as much granulated sugar as you like. Place the cookies on a cookie sheet, either nonstick or lined with parchment paper, and bake in the oven at 375 degrees for seven to eight minutes.

Beltane—May 1

PART VI

Litha—June 19–22

Litha is also known as midsummer or the summer solstice. It represents the time of fulfillment. Midsummer is one of the significant turning points in the year. The sun is in the highest point in the sky. We celebrate the earth in all her full glory, but it is also a time for the realization that change is inevitable and anticipation of the harvest to come.

The Battle of the Oak King and Holly King represents the symbolic battle between summer—the Oak King—and winter—the Holly King and happens twice a year, on the two solstices. On the summer solstice, when the Oak King is stronger, he wins, ushering in a season of growth and fertility. On the other hand, the Holly King will prevail on the winter solstice, leading us into winter, rest, and transformation. In some traditions, the Oak King and the Holly King are seen as dual aspects of The Horned God. Each of these twin aspects rules for half the year, battles for the favor of the Goddess, then retires to nurse his wounds for the next six months, until it is time for him to reign once more.

Symbols: The sun, roses, sunflowers, honeybees, lightning bugs and water, bonfires, and flowers

Activities: Stay up on Midsummer's Eve and watch the sunrise, greet the light, watch the sun go down in the evening, meditate and look back at the past season, and set your goals for the season ahead.

Incense: Lemon, myrrh, pine, rose, wisteria, and cedar

Spell Work: Empowerment, healing, self-love, fire spells, and candle magick

Deities: Freya, Flora, Aine, Lugh, the Green Man, Bast, Brigid, and Pan

Gemstones: Emerald, aventurine, jade, citrine, topaz, amber, and tiger's eye

Trees, Fruits, and Herbs: Mugwort, chamomile, oak, honeysuckle, berries, and ivy

Animals: Horse, cow, bee, butterfly, robin, and wren

Colors: Yellow, gold, green, red, and black

Working with Wishing Stones

Have you ever walked along the shore and found a rock with a white line running all around it? Legend says that you've found a wishing stone.

They can be found almost everywhere, like at the beach, but where I live the whole city is overloaded with river rocks. You see houses here with river-rock chimneys, walls, rocks around flower beds, you name it. River rocks are rocks that have been worn and rounded by the action of moving water. While wishing rocks are often found on riverbeds and beaches, not all river rocks have the markings of a wishing stone.

It's believed that wishing stones don't belong to us. Think of them as little spirits who come into your life temporarily to help, whom you then release so they can help someone else. Litha is a great time to use wishing stones, as it is a time for manifestation and looking forward.

One way of working with them is that after finding the stone, you go to the seashore, make a wish, and throw the stone into the ocean.

Another way to work with wishing stones is to trace your finger around the line. Keep your eyes closed while you do this and make a wish. You can then either throw the stone into the sea, trying your best to throw it as hard as you can, or you can give it to another person. If you do either of these things, your wish will come true.

It's also said that if you make a wish on behalf of someone else, perhaps a friend or family member, then all your own wishes will come true.

Another method for working with a wishing stone is to go to a remote location where there are no houses or people. Hold the stone tightly in your left hand, warming it. Close your eyes and say your wish out loud while turning the stone over and over, focusing your intention into the stone. Switch the stone to your right hand, then throw it as hard as you can to the east.

Creating a Personal Pentagram of Intent

A pentagram, a five-pointed star, is one of the most famous symbols of witchcraft. Enter any metaphysical shop or new age store and you're sure to see a plethora of them. But did you know you could create your own personal pentagram to set your intention? The pentagram is an ancient symbol with many different meanings, but most importantly, it has long been believed to be a potent protection against evil and negative energy. It's a symbol that shields both the wearer and the home. It is also frequently used as a sigil, which is an inscribed or painted symbol considered to have magickal power. A pentagram can be created and used all throughout the Wheel of the Year, and Litha is a great time to create and use one because of the strong magickal and mystical properties of the sabbat.

Litha—June 19–22

Traditionally, the pentagram's five angles have been attributed to the five metaphysical elements of the ancients.

Earth: Represents stability and physical endurance

Fire: Represents courage and daring

Water: Represents emotions and intuition

Air: Represents intelligence and the arts

Spirit: Represents the all and the divine

The pentagram may be surrounded by a circle, representing the continual flow of life or energy. (When enclosed within a circle, this symbol is known as a pentacle.) The number five has traditionally been regarded as mystical and magickal and is considered to be under the influence of Mars. Some think of the five-pointed star within the circle as force or power contained and controlled by divine wisdom.

When used in ritual, pentagrams are drawn to set a witch's protection and positive power, and are used to control the elements. Commonly drawn in the air with a wand or athame, the starting point varies from tradition to tradition and according to uses or intent. The important part is that the pentagram be drawn in one continuous motion and never be broken.

I always wear a pentagram, but I had a thought about utilizing the pentagram in an even more personal way. It's the belief in the power of the pentagram and the intent put into creating it that gives it power. Keep that essence of the pentagram and add another layer to it by creating a personalized pentagram of intent, which allows us to work with the pentagram to acquire the things that we, specifically and individually, need and want in our lives. What these things are will vary from person to person—it could be love, financial security, or protection. What's important is that you identify five elements of *personal importance*.

To create your personalized pentagram, first be aware and respectful of the original elements of earth, air, water, fire, and spirit. Then add the five elements that you have chosen as being important to you. For example:

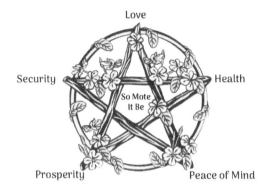

There are no hard rules for creating your pentagram. Make it as complex or simple as you like. You can draw it on a piece of paper or craft one out of whatever materials you wish. In a pinch, you can even grab your athame, wand, or even use your index finger to draw it in the air, calling out the five points you've chosen.

If you chose to make it tangible, the pentagram must be charged and activated. The easiest way to charge it is to hold it in your hand and charge it with your energy. Close your eyes and visualize sending energy down your arms to your hands and out from your fingertips into the pentagram. You can also carve the symbol into a candle and allow the candle to burn down, gently bang a meditative gong, or ring a prayer or altar bell. Don't be afraid to use your own preferred method of charging and activating, if you have one.

After your pentagram has been charged and activated, keep it on your altar or someplace where it won't be disturbed. You can make more than one, if need be. Some people's needs are greater than others, but don't worry. One pentagram will not cancel out the other.

Some pentagrams will be made specifically to be ongoing for months or even years, while others might be for short-term use. Once they are activated, they will work indefinitely. When the time comes that your personal pentagram has served its purpose, you can release its energies and neutralize it. You can do this by closing your eyes and imagining it as a bright ball of light. Focus your intention on it and say, "I release and neutralize your energy," and then imagine the bright ball of light growing dimmer and dimmer until it goes out completely. Once it has been extinguished, don't forget to thank the universe for answering the call.

Litha Spells
Bright Summer Solstice/Litha
On June 21st we celebrate the longest day of the year. It is a time of abundance, growth, and light. We light bonfires or candles to celebrate the light and warmth of the sun. Here is a simple spell to celebrate the beginning of summer without having to build a bonfire.

You will need:

- A yellow or gold candle

- Frankincense or sandalwood incense

- A small bowl of water

- A pinch of salt

- A flower that represents the colors of summer like sunflower, yellow rose, marigold, and chrysanthemum

- A crystal of tiger's eye, carnelian, citrine, amber, onyx, or jade

- A piece of yellow or orange fruit of your choice, like lemon, orange, or mango

You can do this spell indoors or out, but if you can't go outside, find a place near a window that brings in natural light.

Take a couple of cleansing breaths, and light the candle and incense. Put salt into the water, place the crystal, flower, and fruit next to the water, then recite the following incantation:

Salt is to purify, water is to cleanse.
The crystals have great properties, on that you can depend.
Flowers and fruit represent growth for the season.
We put all this together for a very important reason.

136   *Magick for All Seasons*

May the energy of the sun shine down upon me
To brighten my days.
So Mote It Be

Take a moment to think about that positive energy coming your way. Let the incense burn, blow out the candle, sit down, and enjoy your piece of fruit.

Then pour the salt water outside, giving it back to the earth, and when the flower wilts, take it outside and back to the earth as well. Keep the crystal close by.

Summer Magick Spell Jar

Summer is the season of nature's abundance, and it's time to enjoy its prosperity. Go out and gather bits and pieces of objects in nature that catch your eye. When put together, this jar will serve you well during this season and the rest of the year as well.

You will need:

- A glass jar with a lid, any size of your choice, depending on what you're going to put in it

Here is a list of items to help get you started, but use your imagination and make the jar your own:

- **Herbs:** Thyme, dill, basil, rosemary, mint, oregano, bay leaf, and cinnamon stick

- **Stones:** Green aventurine, moonstone, aquamarine, rose quartz, and sunstone

- **Incense:** Chamomile, ginger, rose, cedar, sandalwood, sage, and lavender

- **Other:** Sea shells from the beach, shiny pennies, pretty pebbles, fallen twigs or leaves, blades of grass, sunflower seeds, watermelon seeds, a feather a bird left behind, and rose petals

Gather your items and place them in your jar. Before you close the lid, hold the jar in your hands and recite this incantation:

Litha—June 19–22

The warmth of summer is in this jar,
With items that came from near and far.
May it bring me abundance this time of year
And brighten up the atmosphere.
When the cold of winter has come about,
May it warm my soul, day in and day out.
So Mote It Be

Put the lid on the jar and set in on a windowsill or anyplace in the house that it can get some daily sun to keep it charged.

Bug Potion #9

Love Potion #9 is all well and good when you want to draw someone to you, but sometimes you need to keep things—like mosquitos, gnats, and other biting little critters—far away. When it's summertime and the bugs are biting, there are lots of over-the-counter bug sprays out there, but this is an easy way to make your own that will keep those biting bugs away.

You will need:

- 16-ounce jar with a lid

- A small spray bottle

- 2 tablespoons chopped fresh mint, basil, and lavender leaves

- 1 cup boiling water

- 1 cup witch hazel or isopropyl alcohol

Steep the herbs in the jar of boiling water until cooled. Strain, and add one cup of witch hazel or alcohol to the jar. Close the lid and shake while reciting the following incantation:

This potion will keep insects away
With just a spritz both night and day.
I'll be happy and bite-free.
Those biters will be avoiding me.
So Mote It Be

Transfer the potion into the spray bottle and spritz as needed.

You can make different sprays using other herb combinations that repel bugs like basil, bay leaves, catnip, mint, sage, thyme, or peppermint. It's always a good idea to test the spray for possible allergic reactions before using it more liberally. Swab a little bit of your Bug Potion #9 on the inside of your arm and wait forty-eight hours to make sure you have no adverse reaction to it.

Emotional-Healing Spell

Candle therapy is an ancient healing method used by various cultures and spiritual traditions. The energy emitted by the candle is combined with visualization and meditation. You can heal your emotions by taking control; it's easier than you think. Trust in yourself, and you will make it happen.

You will need:

- A small light-blue candle

- Incense or essential oils such as lavender, ylang-ylang, sandalwood, frankincense, clary sage, or chamomile

Light the candle and the incense, or if you're using essential oil, anoint the candle. Then take three deep cleansing breaths and repeat the following incantation:

My emotions are black clouds over my head.
They linger there with intense power causing me dread.
I've had enough; it's time to fight back.
I see the clouds that I will attack.
I'm in control and see the clouds now slowly shrink away.
With all my might I'll win this fight and things will be okay.
I'll count to three and then I'll see the clouds just disappear.
Here we go. One, two three. It's gone! I'm free and clear!
So Mote It Be

Let the candle and incense burn out.

Litha—June 19–22

Bottle Spell to Get a Raise

Unfortunately, adults don't get the summer off. Even in the best of times, it's often difficult to ask for a raise, but with the cost of living going sky high these days, don't be afraid to speak up. In addition to asking for a raise, this bottle spell will help you get whatever else you need.

You will need:

- An empty glass jar or bottle

- Five of the following items: pennies, dimes, quarters, kernels of dried corn (unpopped popcorn will work), sesame seeds, cinnamon sticks, cloves, pecans, and whole allspice

Place each into the bottle and close it tightly. Shake the bottle for a moment or two while reciting the following incantation:

Silver, spice, herbs, and copper,
Blend together to increase my coffer.
Doing this will be a good deed,
To bring in the money that I most certainly need.
So Mote It Be

Place the bottle on a table somewhere in the house, preferably where you keep your purse, wallet, or checkbook when you are at home.

Leadership Quartz Crystal Spell

Maybe you've just gotten a job promotion that includes leadership capabilities, or any other circumstance where you suddenly find yourself in charge. It may be intimidating when you find yourself in this situation, so here's a spell to help you give it your all.

You will need:

- An owl amulet (or a picture of an owl if you don't have an amulet)

- A bay leaf

- A clear quartz crystal

- A small silver box

Write the words *patience, success, focus,* and *effectiveness* on the bay leaf and place it in the box. Put the owl amulet in next and then the quartz. Before closing the box, repeat the following incantation:

> Owl, bestow on me the wisdom that I shall need
> To do a good job and learn how to lead.
> May the words on the bay leaf jump into action
> And let me proceed with no undue distraction.
> Quartz, grant me clever thought, power, and clarity
> To do my job with abundant dexterity.
> So Mote It Be

Close the box and put it somewhere easily accessible so, until you are comfortable in your new position, you'll be able to place your hands on the box and repeat the incantation for an energy boost.

Fourth of July Sparkling Wish Spell

With the bright lights and sounds of fireworks, use this time to harness that energy and make a wish. Even though this seems to be a very simple spell, it is as powerful as the fireworks that fill the sky.

You will need:

- A sparkler

Gather your thoughts, light the sparkler, and use it like a pen to write your wish in the air. When you're done writing, raise the sparkler pointing up to the sky as it burns itself out and recite this incantation:

> Bright light in the night,
> Carry my wishes with all of your might
> Into the ethers a place that's enchanted,
> Where wishes are born and oftentimes granted.
> The energy and power that fill the air
> Have the strength to get them there.
> Please hear my wish and make it come true.
> This is what I ask of you.
> So Mote It Be

Litha—June 19–22

You can measure and burn a sparkler beforehand to see how long it lasts. That will give you some idea of how much time you have to write your wish before it burns out. A four-inch sparkler burns about twenty to twenty-five seconds, a seven-inch burns for forty seconds, a ten-inch burns for sixty seconds, and a fourteen-inch, about seventy seconds.

Calming Your Pet on the Fourth of July

The Fourth of July, with all its fireworks, is the one of the noisiest times of the year in the United States. The loud noises can easily spook our animal friends. Some pets seem not to be bothered with the loud and endless bangs, but others get very scared and need some calming.

You will need:

- An aquamarine, lace agate, rhodonite, or moonstone crystal

After you consecrate the stone with salt water or charge it under the last full moon, take the stone in your hand and pour your healing energy into it. If you can hold your pet while you charge the stone, do so. Otherwise, have them next to you. With the stone in your hand, gently rub it over them while you recite the following incantation:

Anxiety and unrest soon will be gone.
All negativities must be withdrawn.
A sense of relaxation will replace all the fear,
As the stone generates its healing from the front to the rear.
So Mote It Be

It's a good idea to do this spell before the evening gets too loud. You can repeat it as often as needed.

If you have caged critters that react to the noise, do the spell while holding your hand over the cage.

Antianxiety Affirmation

Anxiety and worry are almost a daily occurrence in one way or another, but you don't have to let them get the best of you. Put your defenses in place by sending the anxiety back to the source.

You will need:

- A black candle

- A white candle

The black candle can banish, absorb, and repel negative energies—whether things or people—while a white candle can help protect, heal, and purify.

Light the candles and repeat this incantation:

Hear me, anxiety, it is my aim
To send you back from whence you came.
You're not allowed into my life,
To fill my days with conflict and strife.
My strength and confidence will send you away.
The white light of protection shines both night and day.
Hit the road and now begone.
It's not me that you can call upon.
So Mote It Be

Blow out the candles and watch the smoke carry your anxiety up, up, and away.

To Tell the Truth Spell

July 7th is National Tell the Truth Day! It's the perfect day to cast this spell (maybe to get your neighbors to admit they were the ones shooting off those too-loud fireworks just a few days before). Whenever you get the feeling that you are being lied to, here's an effective spell that will get the truth out of the liar.

You will need:

- A white candle

- A picture of the person (if you don't have a picture, write the person's name on a piece of paper with blue ink)

Put the picture next to the candle and repeat the following incantation:

Litha—June 19–22

I cast this spell to now find out
What your cover-up is all about.
I conjure thee to do what's right,
And I am using all my might
To hear the truth and find out why
It was necessary to tell a lie.
So Mote It Be

As you blow out the candle, say the person's name out loud.

A Midsummer's Dream Spell

Since the dawn of time, it was believed that dreams could give information about the past, present, and future. Ancient Mesopotamians viewed dreams as a form of communication from the gods and kept detailed records of symbols and themes. In modern times, it's not unusual for people to grab their dream dictionaries off the nightstand first thing in the morning to try and figure out the meaning of last night's dream. For those who say they don't dream or can't remember their dreams, give this spell a try.

You will need:

- Lavender, chamomile, clary sage, palo santo, rose, bergamot, or sandalwood incense

Light the incense in your bedroom before you're ready to go to bed and let the incense burn down. Right before you crawl under the covers, recite the following incantation:

Sweet scents that fill the air, let me sleep without a care.
I want to know day by day, what my dreams have to say.
And when I wake up in the morning light,
My recollection will be bright.
So Mote It Be

Release the Anger

There are times when the anger builds up so much you think you're going to pop. Here's how to release the anger by popping something else.

You will need:

- One biodegradable balloon for each thing that is making you angry
- A marker
- A pin

Blow up the balloons thinking about what each one represents, then write the name of the person or situation that made you so mad on the balloon and recite the following incantation:

My anger's now in this balloon,
And I will release it very soon.
I'm getting rid of all the strife
By popping it now out of my life.
Let the feeling be taken away.
Up in the air is where it will stay.
I will do it on the count of three,
And then I will be anger-free.
So Mote It Be

Take the balloon(s) outside and as you count to three, visualize the anger floating away. Then, with the pin, pop the balloon.

The Healing Bubble

This spell can be used for yourself and for others. All it takes is visualization and a strong intent. If it is for others, you will be sending the healing energy remotely. You will need nothing in the way of tools, but feel free to light a candle or burn some incense of your choice.

Find a quiet spot where you won't be interrupted. Get comfortable, then take three deep cleansing breaths.

Litha—June 19–22

For self-healing, close your eyes and visualize that you are now surrounded by a large, clear bubble. You feel safe and comfortable inside. There's a light breeze and wisps of gold float all around you. That is healing energy.

For remote healing, visualize that person surrounded by the bubble.

If the healing is for something physical, zone in on the part of the body that needs attention. If it's not physical, focus on the problem that needs healing. Once you've pinpointed the need, repeat the following incantation:

If this healing is on yourself:

I need help on the double,
And trust in the power of this bubble.
As I sit here, it's my intent
To heal the ailment that is my torment.
I will feel the energy taking away
The condition upon me this very day.
I'm thankful for the powers that now hear my plea
And allow me this healing.
So Mote It Be

If you're remote healing:

I need help on the double,
And trust in the power of this healing bubble.
As I sit here, it's my intent
To heal the ailment that is [name's] torment.
[Name] will feel the energy taking away
The condition upon [him/her/them] this very day.
I'm thankful for the powers that now hear my plea
And allow me this healing.
So Mote It Be

Concentrate on what you want to heal and visualize a bright cleansing light forming in the bubble. The energy of the white light will show you that your healing has been received.

The Magick Traveling Bag

When my friend Sam Miller is away from home, she, like Mary Poppins, is never without her traveling bag. It contains all the necessary tools of the trade that a clever witch might need at the spur of the moment. Although she didn't grab a coat rack, I was amazed at the number of items she did pull out of that small bag.

A Seasoned Witch's Traveling Bag for Meandering Enchantments

by Sam Miller

Any water witch worth her salt—her sea salt—won't be too long away from the source of her well-being. If one should reside some miles from the ocean, a journey along the coast is a euphoric necessity. The time spent traveling is a time of renewal and wonderment, and there is absolutely no reason for you to leave your craft behind.

Going on a road trip? Off for a weekend with a few like-minded sisters? Hot-footing it to an unknown destination? Just want to feel a little more secure and protected? Grab your little bag of magick on your way out the door.

It doesn't require a well-honed proficiency in spell work to put together a traveling altar bag. All it requires is that you really want one. Be a timid beginner or a contented crone like myself, everything you need to manifest it is already in your heart and mind. After all, this is your own magick.

Packing with a Purpose
Finding your bag.

Selecting a traveling pouch can be as simple or complicated as you choose to make it. I know practitioners that use fanny packs, knapsacks, small carpet bags, and even paper bags if they are headed out on the run. Craft one yourself or if you have no flair for that sort of thing, like myself, find someone to design and make one for you. Just remember in your zeal to get going that one most important requirement is that it should be easy to carry. I opted for a small carpet-bag type. It has two clutch handles, a sturdy zipper opening that allows the bag to expand, and most importantly, it is ringed with pockets. Find yourself one that is well-made and will stand up to travel: being tossed in car seats, corners, being dusted with ash, oil, candle wax, and dirt. In simple terms, find one that you will entrust to hold all your magickal workings safely. One you have confidence in. Find a friend.

Now ritual work can be as complex or as plain and unadorned as you like. When you're on the move, simplicity often takes precedence. It does for me. Yet that by no means diminishes my ritual or casting. Over my crone-laden years, I have embellished my travelling altar with a good many accoutrements, all of which were geared towards my personal working elements of water and wind.

I have at the ready:

- A small altar cloth because you just never know
- A small cauldron and stand for incense and small burning spells
- Parchment, ink, and pen for spells, summoning, banishing, or lists
- A lightweight wooden mortar and pestle for mixing and reducing
- An offering dish for gifts and cookies
- Spoons to measure and stir
- A bronze sea star for my pentagram because why not?
- A tiny pendulum board and pendulum for advice from a voice other than my own
- Small box of bay leaves and tiny sea stars—an easy way to send off a spell
- Tea lights for all the obvious reasons
- Incense, stick or loose, for cleansing (but try not to set off the smoke alarms in the hotel room)
- Candle scribe for inscribing on wax
- Fiber twine for binding of candles
- Assorted salts (My arsenal includes salts of all sorts for specific and mundane uses. Terrific protection.)

- Assorted spices and herbs for a little umph to those spells
- Oracle ocean cards or just oracle or tarot

Deciding what you need for your basics is totally a matter of personal preference. What is it you personally require to do meaningful and heartfelt crafting? Are you bounded with a particular style of divination? Or are you a delightfully eclectic soul that plays out the magick as the moment beckons?

I always include a deck of cards, often oracle and sometimes tarot. It's a handy and quick way to get advice when you're in a quandary, or just not sure how to proceed. Add a pendulum with a small board and a few shells for tossing, tiny candles for reading flames or wax on water, and even a small mirror. Go with what you know!

I like having another voice. Things you'll tuck inside your little traveling bag of magick will become like friends and their advice will become more useful the more times you use them.

Carrying your tools can be secretive or done with pride. Yes, I have a small bag filled to the gunnels with devices for casting and comfort on my travels. But I also have a method of toting those same exact gizmos out quite boldly, in the light of day.

When doing public sea witchery or giving talks at museums or libraries, I carry my craft spread across my chest and hips in a specifically custom fashioned leather baldric. Yes, just like the pirates used to wear. Only this particular model is strung with wee loops to hold vials of salts, sharks' teeth, urchin spines, and herbs. It also has bronze rings for clipping larger bottles in small leather harnesses, an attached leather box for pendulums and coins, clips to hold small, shell-bound paper grimoires, a compass, a pouch for candles, and whatever the day might require. I always walk a bit prouder in my magickal rig.

Why do I bother? I could give you loads of enchanting reasons, however, I think I'll give you an example instead.

Carmel by the Sea is the place that nurtures my soul, soothes my spirit, and where I find true magick around every turn. In the trees and shoreline are persuasive reasons to believe in those things we feel, but cannot see. You can feel it in the breeze that brushes your face, the smell of the sea air and even in the shade of the cypress trees. Magickal life is there.

I have so many longtime friends there and some, like myself, are practitioners of the old ways.

I never travel up to the central coast of California with casting in mind, but always take my traveling alter, not only out of habit, but out of hope for the unexpected.

My last visit was in June of 2023. It was long overdue and I was eager to spend time with a friend of over thirty years, Cheryl Gillette. She is a child actors' studio manager, and seasoned witch. Over the course of a few days, I became aware that she was in need of finding new housing because, as a caregiver, the place that she was presently calling home was no longer suitable.

I suggested that we hold a small rite in my hotel room just to get the ball rolling for her, help to move to distractions and blockages out of the way, and find her some help. And, you guessed it, my travel altar was sitting on the bed just waiting to be used.

This is where you begin to fashion your inherent magickal wiles. My larder was a bit lean but the basics were there and ready for whatever we might require of them.

- Alter clock—check
- 4 tea light candles for the corners—present
- Larger candle to represent Hestia, goddess of hearth and home—yep
- Starfish pentacle—absolutely
- Crystals from her altar at home—done
- A mix of cinnamon, coffee grounds, lavender, and sugar to hasten and sweeten the deal (much of which was gathered from the hotel's freebies)
- Wine and chocolates for the offering—oh, you betcha.

The candles were lit and the quarters called. Hestia was invited to our circle and she came in with quite a roar.

"New, loving home" was inscribed on the Hestia candle and placed on the dish with herbs. Supplications were made for the needed help to move forward. Requests to remain on the peninsula and much conversation was had.

Hestia really was a presence to be reckoned with but oh so comforting. Wine was offered and shared; chocolate caramel patties were devoured amid happy discussions as if talking to an old friend. Thanks were given, the quarters released, the circle closed, and Hestia lingered. Travel altar was set right and packed away with care and gratitude.

The next day, a real estate agent that I had talked to the last year contacted me out of the blue to see if it was near time that I wanted to move up to the peninsula. Well duh! No, I'm not quite ready yet, but I explained my friend's situation and the real estate agent completely took over the legwork and even sent his own assistant to help prepare her house to sell. Like a gift from a goddess, he swooped in and has been her savior.

Ah, travel altar you've done me proud.

Candle Magick Is Easy

With safety as your first concern, there is little that can't be trussed up into a successful candle spell. It is why I carry small candles in my traveling altar: three- to five-inch tall pillars in assorted colors. Need to know the truth about someone's intentions? Looking for who the toxic influence in a relationship might be? Want to burn that bridge for good and all? Want to bind or protect your pets? Easy peasy.

Stock up on:

- A flat, fireproof dish and/or small bowl
- Beach sand
- Candles of different colors, pillars about three to five inches tall
- Twine
- Sea salt, Himalayan pink salt, elemental salts (earth, water, fire, and air)
- Four basic herbs you could gather (your preference but herbs such as parsley, cilantro, dill, and oregano are easily gathered from the supermarket)

Litha—June 19–22

- For specialized rites, you can gather less common herbs as desired or directed.
- Parchment and pen
- Almond or olive oil

This is extremely customizable spell work.

It can be used to distance someone you're uncomfortable with or to break off a relationship. It can manifest information about someone's intentions or help you sort out a troublemaker. With just slight variations in tying the twine, herbal choices, salts, and candle colors, there will be magick afoot.

First, find your intention; without it, any spell is rudderless. Be honest with yourself because magick will bounce back on a deceiver. Work wisely and for the good. Casting is done with and from the heart. Ground yourself, be sincere and truthful, and the unseen potentials of nature will respond.

Second, prepare your plate or bowl with a layer of sand deep enough to hold the candles upright. Working with intent, pour a layer of black salts in a circle. The two candles stand inside this circle, so make it an adequate size. Sprinkle some whole cloves about the circle.

You'll need two candles. Choose a color to represent yourself and a dark blue for your suspected evil doer. Carve "They who are deceiving" into the blue candle. Dress (anoint) both the candles with almond or olive oil. Now dress or roll the blue candle in black pepper and your candle in lavender, mugwort, or pure sea salt. Place both candles in the salt circle of the dish about two to three inches apart.

Cut a small piece of twine and tie it between the two candles about one third of the way down. The intent you put into the construction of this spell should be sufficient so that no incantation is required, but you do you. If it empowers your work or makes you more comfortable, by all means, incant away!

Circle the plate with incense to cleanse, then light both candles, and watch them burn. See from which candle the twine burns and falls first. Let them burn down until they are extinguished. If your candle burns out first, you are mistaken about the ill intent from this individual. If the blue candle

152   *Magick for All Seasons*

burns down first, they are indeed a source of mischief but the mix of black pepper and herbs will mute them in short order.

Want a bit of protection for yourself or your pet?

Pour a circle of white salt on a small dish. In the center, place a sigil or some sage. On a whole bay leaf write "I am protected" or "My cat Ichabod is protected," or whoever it is that you're looking out for. Dress a black candle in oil and roll it along the bay leaf until the candle is wrapped in it. Secure with twine. Use a flame to soften the bottom of the candle and secure the center of the plate or bowl. Circle the candle with incense and light the candle. Watch it burn until extinguished.

One word more . . .

Traveling altars are empowering, enticing physical reminders of who we are. Having the accoutrements of our Craft at hand is joyful. Fun even! However, I'd like to leave you with the reminder that everything you need to manifest intent is already with you. All that is required is your intent, your heart, and your hands. Magick is the embodiment of your individuality, your substance, your conscience, and your essence. Working with all that nature supplies gives focus and added power to the things we would beckon and entice into our lives. Yet the preeminent power is within you. You.

So gather your stores, your traveling bag, and be wistful in your wanderings. Work at your Craft and be of help to others. Be Blessed.

You are the magick!

Litha Recipes
Summer Fruit Salad

I love summer salads, especially when they have a simple but delicious sweet dressing. You can choose your own combination of your favorite fruit, but here's the recipe I like the best.

banana
pineapple
apples
grapes
blueberries

Litha—June 19–22

blackberries
8 or 16 ounces of sour cream (Depends on how much fruit you
are using.)
brown sugar
cinnamon
a drop of vanilla extract

Cut fruit into bite-sized pieces, then mix together in a bowl. Cover the bowl and place it in the refrigerator while you're making the dressing.

Put the sour cream in a bowl and sprinkle in the brown sugar a bit at a time. Combine thoroughly until the sugar melts in and you've got the desired sweetness.

Add cinnamon to taste, then add a drop or two of vanilla. Mix it all together and you're done! Fruit salad is also delicious without the dressing.

Conjured Shredded Chicken in Chili Verde

With all due respect to Lucky Charms, this dish is magickally delicious.

1 pound tomatillos
20 black peppercorns
6 fresh cloves
3 or 4 cloves garlic
½ small onion, roughly chopped
1 tablespoon oregano
1 cup fresh cilantro, chopped
salt to taste
a couple tablespoons of oil
1 cooked chicken, shredded

Add all ingredients, except the chicken, into a blender and blend until smooth.

Pour the oil into a frying pan. Add the blended sauce and simmer on low for thirty minutes.

When the sauce is done, add the shredded chicken and mix well.

154   *Magick for All Seasons*

A Blink of the Eye Hawaiian Pie

This pie really does only take a few minutes, or blinks, to prepare. One bite and you'll feel like you're on vacation in an island paradise.

1 can crushed pineapples, undrained (20 ounces)
1 box instant vanilla pudding mix (6 servings)
8 ounces sour cream
1 9-inch graham cracker crust
1 can pineapple slices (8 ounces)
8 maraschino cherries
½ cup sweetened, flaked coconut
whipped cream or a small container of nondairy whipped
    topping for piping

In a large bowl, combine crushed pineapple with its syrup, dry pudding mix, and sour cream. Mix until well combined. Spoon into the pie crust and decorate top with pineapple slices and cherries. Sprinkle with coconut.

Cover and chill at least two hours before serving.

It's delicious as is, but a dollop of nondairy whipped topping or fresh whipped cream might make it even better.

PART VII

Lughnasadh/Lammas—August 1

Lughnasadh and Lammas, both celebrated on August 1st, are now often syncretized with each other. Lughnasadh is the Irish festival that marks the beginning of the harvest season, and Lammas (from an Old English word meaning "loaf mass"), also known as Loaf Mass Day, is a Christian festival dedicated to the blessing of the first-fruits harvest, although it may derive from earlier, pre-Christian British traditions. Today, many Pagans and witches celebrate Lammas as a sabbat.

This is the festival of sacrifice and is the first of the three Celtic harvest festivals. Now is the time that we, too, reap the harvest of our own seeds that were sown at Imbolc. The god personifies the spirit of nature that dies each autumn. Willingly cut down, he is a sacrifice for the sake of the living, while the goddess is the principle of eternal life. His spirit descends into the earth, the womb of the goddess, waiting to be reborn at Yule.

By celebrating Lughnasadh as a harvest holiday, we honor our ancestors and the hard work they must have had to do in order to survive. We give thanks for the abundance we have in our lives and are grateful for the food on our tables. Lammas is a time of transformation, rebirth, and new beginnings.

In some Wiccan and modern Pagan traditions, it is also a day of honoring Lugh, the Celtic craftsman god. He is a deity of many skills and was honored in various aspects throughout the British Isles, as well as in Europe. Lughnasadh (pronounced Loo-NAHS-ah) is still celebrated in many parts of the world today.

Symbols: Corn dollies, wheat, bread, cauldron, corn, herbs, threshing tools, lambs, and dough

Activities: Create corn dollies, make fresh breads and pastries, and have a bonfire

Incense: Rose, sandalwood, and copal

Spell Work: Prosperity

Deities: Ceres, Danu, Hestia, Lugh, and Vesta

Gemstones: Amber, citrine, aventurine, and carnelian

Trees, Fruits, and Herbs: Rosemary, poppy, basil, sunflower, cornstalk, and barley

Animal: Calf, crow, pig, rooster, chicken, and goat

Color: Brown, green, orange, yellow, gold, and beige

Crafting a Rustic Magick Wand

There are many factors to consider when choosing the perfect wood for your magick wand or staff. It's my belief that to make a wand the wood should never be cut. It should be found, dropped from a living tree.

Once you've got the branch you must consecrate it to cleanse it from old energies. It can be as simple as running it through sacred smoke. I've heard that some have used a quartz crystal as well. They hold the crystal above the wood and envision it absorbing the negative energies released from the wood.

Scrape off the bark, then carve the stick into a wand and sand it to make it smooth. Decorate it any way you wish.

Types of Wand/Staff Woods and Their Properties

Alder
Personality: Bold
Primary Use: Magick involving the fair folk

Apple

Personality: Gentle and relaxed
Primary Use: Nature magick

Ash

Personality: Assertive
Primary Use: Transfiguration

Birch

Personality: Creative
Primary Use: Charms

Box Elder

Personality: Adventurous
Primary Uses: Transfiguration and alchemy

Cedar

Personality: Good-natured
Primary Use: All forms of white magick

Cherry

Personality: Optimistic and loving
Primary Use: Divination

Cypress

Personality: Reflective and communicative
Primary Use: Divination

Elm

Personality: Wise and reliable
Primary Use: Protective magick

Fir
>   Personality: Noble
>   Primary Uses: Healing and potions

Hawthorn
>   Personality: Protective and caring
>   Primary Use: Protective magick

Holly
>   Personality: Inherently good
>   Primary Use: White magick

Ivy
>   Personality: Feminine and strong
>   Primary Uses: Healing and protection

Linden
>   Personality: Strong and artistic
>   Primary Use: Transfiguration

Mahogany
>   Personality: Bold and nature-centered
>   Primary Uses: Weather-calming magick and protective spells

Maple
>   Personality: Adventurous
>   Primary Use: Magick performed at night

Mesquite
>   Personality: Rugged
>   Primary Use: Defensive magick

Oak
Personality: Steadfast
Primary Use: Protective magick

Orange
Personality: Reliable and confident
Primary Use: Combat magick

Pecan
Personality: Driven
Primary Uses: Alchemy and potions

Pine
Personality: Strong and quiet
Primary Use: Healing

Plum
Personality: Unrestrained creativity
Primary uses: Transfiguration

Poplar
Personality: Hopeful but grounded
Primary Uses: Divination and dispelling dark magick

Rosewood
Personality: Confident and strong
Primary Use: Love magick

Sycamore
Personality: Curious and vivacious
Primary Use: No specialty

Vinewood
   Personality: Strong and intelligent
   Primary Uses: Potions and nature magick

Walnut
   Personality: Expansive
   Primary Uses: Weather and travel magick

Willow
   Personality: Relaxed and feminine
   Primary Use: Divination

Yew
   Personality: Strong and independent
   Primary Use: Divination

Yucca
   Personality: Light but strong
   Primary Use: Healing

Creating a Manifestation Box

Do you feel there's something missing from your life but you're not sure how to obtain it? Try creating a manifestation box. A manifestation box is a powerful law-of-attraction tool used to bring your desires to life. The law of attraction states that like attracts like. If you think positive thoughts, you will attract positive energy and vice versa. You can use the law of attraction to literally attract your desires. Remember: Where energy flows, that's where attention goes.

By using a manifestation box, you are sending an affirmation and intention to the universe. It works to bring your dreams into reality.

You will need:

- An intention

- A box

- Paper and pen

- Objects related to your intention (For example: If you are in need of financial aid, put the largest denomination of paper money in your possession into the box to attract wealth.)

Creating a manifestation box is simple. Choose a box to your liking—make sure it's big enough to hold the items you've selected related to your intention. You can decorate the box with personal symbols or pictures related to what you wish to achieve. Set an intention and place the objects in the box. Add pictures, sentimental objects, a wish written on a piece of paper, crystals, feathers, symbols, and anything else that you consider lucky or sacred. The idea is to fill the box with things that radiate the energy of your manifestations. These special items will amplify the energy within the box.

You can use your manifestation box to manifest one specific element into your life or you can use it as an ongoing manifestation tool. The main point is that you know exactly what you want to manifest. Once you make up your mind about what you want to manifest, the first thing you should put in the box is a letter of intent to the universe. The letter should be positive and uplifting. Do not come from a place of desperation and negativity. Instead, thank the universe for everything it has already done for you and thank it in advance for making your manifestations come true. If you send positive energy towards your intentions, they will be more likely to come to life. Remember: Like attracts like.

As you place each item in the box, envision that your intention has become a reality. There are times, just as in spell work, that what you wish for may not come true. This usually means that this is not the proper time for that to happen, or perhaps that you're wishing for something that may not be good for you in the long run. Remember, the universe has your back and sometimes needs to step in and alter things for your own good. Trust in the universe.

Lughnasadh/Lammas—August 1

There is no right or wrong way to use or make a manifestation box, but the more you work with your box, the greater chance you have of receiving the universal blessings you deserve.

Just keep in mind that *thoughts* become *things*.

Lughnasadh/Lammas Spells
Magickal Harvest Jar

Although it is still summer, autumn is just around the corner, and the harvest season is just beginning. On the night of Lammas, create a jar to plant the wishes that you'd like to harvest. You can make this a personal jar, or one that the whole family can take part in.

You will need:

- Frankincense, cinnamon, meadowsweet, or sandalwood incense

- A pretty jar with a lid or cork

- Sage leaves

- Wishing grains like oats, barley, carraway seeds, rice, or corn (popcorn will do)

- Hazelnuts or other nuts in the shell

- Pen and paper

- Yellow ribbon

Light the incense and add all the ingredients to the jar, then write the wishes on pieces of paper, roll them up, tie each one with a ribbon, and place them in the jar. Before you close the jar, repeat the following incantation:

In order to harvest, we first must plant seeds.
These items we've gathered will help with our needs.
May each wish be harvested all in good time,
And the end results be oh, so sublime.
So Mote It Be

164   *Magick for All Seasons*

Seal the jar and place it somewhere where it can't be disturbed.

Burning Bowl Ritual

The Wheel of the Year keeps turning. Lughnasadh/Lammas is August Eve and is the first of three harvest festivals. Many Pagans celebrate the bounty of the earth and give thanks for what we have. Focus on an abundance of something you might need in your life, but this is also a time of letting go of things that no longer serve you.

Once we get rid of our unwanted baggage, we make room for an abundance of good things to come. This is a ritual of letting go, cleansing, and good intentions. The most important thing when it comes to making this a successful spell is to sit down and seriously think about everything you can now do without. This could mean an annoying habit, personal items that are now useless, people in your lives whose friendship or love have faded away . . . anything in your life that you now see as a waste of time, whether it be thoughts, items, or people. Don't be afraid to sit in your feelings when it comes to letting go of things you no longer need; this can be very difficult. Think long and hard and make a clearheaded decision.

You will need:

+ Incense of your choice

+ A pen with green ink

+ Paper

+ A fireproof bowl

Find a quiet place where you won't be disturbed. Light the incense and write your list of those things that no longer serve you. After each thing you write, close your eyes and, in your mind's eye, see it disappear.

When you're done with your list, put it in the bowl and light it. As the list burns, repeat the following incantation:

Smoke, smoke, please carry away
The things that are useless without delay.
Abundance will come with the turn of the wheel,

Lughnasadh/Lammas—August 1

And then the past will be a done deal.
So Mote It Be

When the list has been charred, take the ashes outside and let the breeze scatter them into the winds.

Simple Money Spell

Money doesn't grow on trees, but you can help your wallet grow in abundance if you do this spell.

You will need:

- A small green crystal

Hold the crystal in your hand and repeat the following incantation:

Precious stone help with my plight,
And hear the words I now recite.
Finances have been running low,
So I ask you to help them grow.
I trust in your ability
To help me with financial stability.
Let new money come my way
Beginning on this very day.
So Mote It Be

You can keep the crystal in your wallet, or when you're home, you can put the crystal on top of your wallet.

Wealth Witch Bottle

Making any kind of bottle spell is just putting things into a jar that align with your spell or intention. You seal your jar with candle wax while holding your intentions in your mind. We all have money on our minds, so this jar is always useful.

You will need:

- A jar with a lid

- Paper and pen

Magick for All Seasons

- A bay leaf
- A basil leaf
- A cinnamon stick
- A penny, a nickel, and a quarter
- A few cloves
- A green candle

Add your items to the jar one at time, then write down your intention, and place it in the jar (like "money, come my way").

Light the candle and repeat this incantation:

Silver, spice, herbs, and copper,
Band together to increase my coffer.
Thanks in advance for the good deed
To bring in the money I most surely need.
So Mote It Be

Seal your jar with candle wax, then place it where you'll see it often to remind you of your intention.

Two Sweet-Smelling Ways to Attract Money

Try using these two simple methods to bring a little bit of extra money you need.

You will need:

Spell Number 1

- An orange
- A dozen whole cloves

Cloves and citrus are great for attracting money and smell wonderful together. Just push the cloves into the skin of the orange and place it into a small bowl or saucer on a table or shelf.

Spell Number 2

· Pumpkin pie spice

Pumpkin pie spice contains cinnamon, cloves, ginger, nutmeg, and allspice. These pieces come together for a powerful money-drawing combination. Place a couple of tablespoons of the spice in small muslin bags and place them here and there throughout the house.

For both of these spells, recite this incantation as you're putting together the ingredients:

Sweet spices when applied
Will keep my wallet satisfied.
May the change in finances get underway
And spring into action this very day.
So Mote It Be

Yes or No Orange Spell

If you need a quick answer to a question that can be answered with yes or no, give this easy divination spell a try.

You will need:

· An orange

· A knife

Hold the orange in your hands and concentrate on the question you need answered for a moment or two, then recite this incantation:

Juicy orange, let me know
Which way that I'm supposed to go.
I'm not sure if it's yes or no.
My thoughts are going to and fro.
The answer lies beneath your rind,
And there my answer I will find.
So Mote It Be

Cut the orange into quarters then count all the seeds. An odd number means no and an even number means yes.

The Money Tree

If there's one thing people need, its money, and since it's illegal to make the counterfeit type, the next best thing is to create a money tree that will attract currency. Be creative. The trees can be big or small and decorated as you wish.

You will need:

- A few fallen branches or twigs (you can also get them at a craft store)
- A vase, bowl, or glass, depending on size of the twigs or branches
- Pebbles, aquarium stones, and coins
- A few strips of material

Place the branches or twigs in the vase or glass and put in enough coins and stones to keep the tree upright, then write your needs or wishes on the strips of material and tie them to the branches. (If it's a tiny tree or you'd rather write down your wishes on a piece of paper and put it under the tree, that will work as well.) When you finish, put some coins around the tree while you repeat the following incantation:

> I made this tree because of need,
> Not created out of greed.
> It's my intent to spend it wisely,
> So I ask you very kindly
> To help me now, I've bills to pay
> And cannot make them go away.
> Now I need you to heed my plea
> And do what you can.
> So Mote It Be

Repeat the incantation daily until your wishes are granted.

Lughnasadh/Lammas—August 1

Money Grows Prosperity Spell

A little bit of magick can help ease big financial burdens. This is a very simple spell, but as the old saying goes, good things come in small packages.

You will need:

- A silver coin

- A tiny flowerpot

- Backyard soil

Before you "plant" the coin, hold it in your hand and repeat the following incantation:

Silver coin, please help me gain
Prosperity to ease the strain.
My finances are in a drought,
So I call on you to help me out.
It's not my intention to rock the boat,
But I need enough to keep myself afloat.
I know you can help me to be worry free.
I've no doubt about it.
So Mote It Be

Plant the coin in a flowerpot or directly in the soil. If it's going into a pot, draw a dollar sign on the pot. If it's going into the soil, place a little marker on a stake with a dollar sign. Envision dollar bills growing out of the pot.

Cat Blessing

I created this spell in honor of International Cat Day, which falls on August 8th. Mark the date and give a blessing to your favorite feline.

You will need:

- A cat-figure candle for each cat you're blessing (or just a white candle if you cannot find a cat candle)

- A stick of incense of your choosing

- Your kitty being with you or somewhere nearby

Light the candle and incense and repeat the following blessing:

> I offer this blessing for you today.
> You've changed my life in a wonderful way.
> I wish you longevity and divine protection
> As I offer you my unconditional affection,
> Blessed Be and I will strive
> To make sure you that you always continue to thrive.
> So Mote It Be

You can use this blessing for any of your pets as well. Simply substitute a plain pillar candle for the cat-shaped candle if you are using it for a different pet. A dog, a snake, even a chinchilla—this spell will bless any and all pets.

Clearing Your Head Invocation

There are days when we really need a clear head and can't settle down. Give this spell a try.

You will need:

- An open mind

- A piece of paper

- A pen with blue ink or any writing implement that writes in blue

Draw a triangle on the piece of paper. Triangles are used for many purposes. In this invocation, the triangle represents the three elements of our being that need to be balanced. They are mind, body, and soul. Focus on your triangle for a moment or two, then recite the following incantation:

> Too many thoughts are in my head,
> Swirling around since I got out of bed.
> Some are important and some are not,
> And some are just an afterthought.

The essential thoughts are free to stay.
The others need to go away.
I need a clear head to do what I must.
All irrelevant thoughts must now bite the dust.
So Mote It Be

Visualize all the unnecessary thoughts in your head disappearing one by one. Repeat the spell as often as you need some clarity.

Meditation to Unclutter Your Mind

There are days when our minds are sharp as a tack and other days we can't remember what we had for dinner the night before. One of the best ways to clear your head is with a simple meditation.

You will need:

- Cinnamon, vanilla, or ginger incense (burning them all at the same time is also an option)

- A clear quartz crystal

- A hematite stone

- A white candle

Find a quiet spot where you won't be disturbed. Light the candle and the incense and hold the crystals in your hand. Take three deep cleansing breaths and recite the following incantation:

My brain is foggy and not up to par.
My thoughts are traveling both near and far.
The incense and stones will unclutter all thought
And help me remember those things I forgot.
So Mote It Be

Close your eyes and stay put for five minutes. Feel the energy of the stones in your hands giving you clarity and let the sweet-smelling incenses untangle your mind.

Floating in Air Morning Affirmation

This is a fun spell, a good way to start the day, and takes less than five minutes. If you're not one of those morning people, you can do this the night before and set your intentions for the day to come.

You will need:

- A stick of incense of your choice that ties in with your intention

Light the stick of incense, then write a few words in the air that will be your intention for the day. For example, if you've got to get up and make a presentation at work and have the jitters, your key words could be "Stay calm." Or if the weather is bad and you have to drive to an appointment, you could say, "Keep me safe." You get the idea.

After you've written your intention, repeat this quick affirmation to seal the deal.

Sacred smoke, do my bidding.
Carry out the request that I'm submitting.
So Mote It Be

Put the incense in a holder and let it burn out.

Flush Your Troubles Away

National Toilet Paper Day is celebrated on August 26th. (See? There really is a day for everything.) Fun fact: The first time toilet paper was sold on a roll in the United States was on August 26, 1871. This is the perfect day to flush your troubles away! This spell is similar to other spells that banish negativity, but unlike the shower spell where you lather up and let the water gently rinse your worries down the drain, flushing wasteful negativity is quite a bit stronger.

You will need:

- Toilet paper

- A pen

Lughnasadh/Lammas—August 1

Write your desire on a piece of toilet paper. If you've got more than one wish, use one square for each. Drop the paper into the toilet and repeat this incantation.

> It's time to flush you out of my life.
> You have given me too much strife.
> As you circle in the bowl,
> I rid you with my heart and soul.
> In my life you were a waste,
> And now your memory will be erased.
> So Mote It Be

Flush the toilet and visualize your troubles going quickly down the drain. (If you have multiple wishes and thus multiple squares of toilet paper, repeat the ritual for each individually.)

Lughnasadh/Lammas Recipes
Corn Pone

A corn pone is a small round loaf, about the size of a biscuit. It is so named because the corn is the main ingredient, and the pone is the shape. They're baked in the oven in a round cast-iron skillet or a baking sheet.

2 cups cornmeal
1 teaspoon salt
2 teaspoons all-purpose flour
2 teaspoons bacon grease
Milk (just enough to make it a stiff batter, about 1 cup)

Mix all the ingredients together, then form the pones by hand and place them on a greased baking sheet.

Bake twelve to fifteen minutes at 425 degrees. The batch bakes about eighteen loaves.

Mystical Rice Pudding

National Rice Pudding Day is August 9th. I tried this rice pudding recipe with brown rice as well, and the nutty tastiness gave it just a bit of a different taste that worked just beautifully. Use either white or brown rice according to your tastes.

2 cups white or brown rice
1 cinnamon stick broken into large pieces
6 cups water
1 can (12 ounces) condensed milk
1 cup raisins
1 teaspoon vanilla
1 cup sugar

Cook the rice and cinnamon stick in the water until all liquid is absorbed and the rice is plump and fluffy.

Stir in the condensed milk, raisins, vanilla, and sugar and simmer over low heat for three to five minutes, mixing occasionally so that the rice doesn't burn.

Serves four to six people.

Charmed Pickled Green Tomatoes

Snow White took a bite of the witch's green apple and went into a deep sleep before she was awakened by the kiss of a handsome prince. I hope your handsome price enjoys a bit of garlic with his kisses because you won't be able to stop eating these perfectly charming pickled green tomatoes.

Green tomatoes: They're not just for frying.

24 green tomatoes
½ cup salt
2 quarts water
1 cup vinegar
6 garlic cloves
2 bay leaves
15 whole peppercorns
1½ teaspoons pickling spice
3 tablespoons dried dill

Wash the tomatoes well and place in a large jar or crock.

Lughnasadh/Lammas—August 1

Bring the remaining ingredients to a boil, set aside to cool for a few minutes, and then pour over the tomatoes, making sure they're completely covered.

Seal the jar and keep in a cool place. Do not refrigerate. It is fine to leave the jar on the kitchen counter but away from the stove for about a week.

The tomatoes can be pickled either whole or cut in half but keep in mind that the halves will require less pickling time.

PART VIII

Mabon—September 19–22

Mabon is the autumn equinox, the second of three harvests, and a time of delicate balance between light and dark. We gather nuts, berries, and fruits of the vine. It heralds the need for valuing, storing, and conserving for the winter ahead. It's a season to recognize our blessings and to honor and thank the goddess and the god. Mabon is the traditional time for celebrations of thanksgiving and harvest festivals. The goddess is the Harvest Queen, but the god's presence is shadowy; he is deep within the underworld. It is said that he is heard in each sigh of the wind and glimpsed in the shades of early dusk. He leads us to the hidden, inward places of our souls and invites us to explore. It is time to make room for contemplation on the quest for balance.

Mabon is considered a time of the mysteries. We honor deities and the spirit world. Considered a time of equilibrium, this is when we stop, relax, and enjoy the fruits of our personal harvests, whether they be from toiling in our gardens, working at our jobs, raising our families, or just coping with the hustle and bustle of everyday life.

Symbols: Cornucopia, pinecone, seeds, and autumn leaves

Activities: Bonfires, and planting seeds and bulbs

Incense: Benzoin, myrrh, sage, pine, and musk

Spell Work: Home protections, releasing negativity, balance, and prosperity

Deities: Mabon, Green Man, Persephone, Morgan, Pomona, and Demeter

Gemstones: Amber, citrine, cat's eye, sapphire, lapis lazuli, and yellow agate

Trees, Fruits, and Herbs: Apple, acorn, yarrow, rosemary, sage, mugwort, and rosehips

Animals: Owl, stag, blackbird, and salmon

Colors: Orange, red, yellow, brown, copper, dark yellow, and dark green

Eye of Newt and Toe of Frog?

"Fillet of a fenny snake, in the cauldron boil and bake. Eye of newt, and toe of frog, wool of bat and tongue of dog. Adder's fork and blind-worm's sting. Lizard's leg and howlet's wing."
—WILLIAM SHAKESPEARE, MACBETH

Conjure up the image of a witch in your mind's eye and you're likely to think of a woman in a pointy black hat standing over a mysterious cauldron full of magick potion. But why do we associate witches with large pots of bubbling brew? The image of a bubbling cauldron being stirred by a witch originates from the large pots in which women used to boil their ingredients to make simples. Simpling was the brewing and distilling of herbs and was practiced by women in most medieval households to keep a very necessary supply of medicinal remedies on hand. During that period, the arts of herbalism, alchemy, and magick were difficult to separate, and the herb women often added the role of spell caster to their role as the dispenser of home-brewed herbal therapies.

One of the most famous examples of witches in literature are the Weird Sisters, the three witches from Shakespeare's *Macbeth* (which some interpret as taking place during autumn) who deliver their fateful prophecy to the titular character. The *Macbeth* witches' famous list of ingredients is thought of as a witch's brew, but did witches back then actually use such ghastly bits and pieces as they stirred their cauldrons? Because witches are closely connected to nature and respect all sentient beings, how in the world did they get away with using bat's wings, cat's foot, and tongue of dog in their potions and brews? The answer is simple. Witches created code names designed to keep magick within the magick circle.

In the Dark Ages, people believed witches were powerful practitioners of evil, so those practicing the Craft needed to devise a way to scare the common folk as a means of protection, and the disturbing names they created stopped non-magickal folk from replicating or sampling their brews. For example, "toe of frog" is really just a buttercup, "wool of bat" is holly leaves, and "tongue of dog" is hound's tongue, which is an herbaceous plant. "Bird's foot" is fenugreek, "calf's snout" is a snapdragon, and "fairy fingers" are foxglove. Many herbalists believe that "eye of newt" refers to mustard seed—as referenced in Marvel's *Agatha All Along*, when a coven of witches brew a magick potion that includes eye of newt.

As the story goes, a coven of witches was so angry with Shakespeare for using real incantations in his play that they put a terrible curse on him, the play, and anyone else who dared utter the word "Macbeth." But is there any evidence of this or is it just an urban legend? Legend has it that the play's first performance, around 1606, was riddled with disaster. The actor playing Lady Macbeth died suddenly, so Shakespeare himself had to take on the part. Other rumored mishaps include a real dagger being used in place of the stage prop for the murder of King Duncan, which resulted in the death of the actor who played the part. To this day, according to a theatrical superstition called The Scottish Curse, speaking the name Macbeth inside a theater, other than as called for in the script while rehearsing or performing, will cause disaster.

Since the beginning of time, mankind has given plants interesting folk names based on certain attributes of the plant, its growth habits, or even specific reasons it was used. The common dandelion has been called bitter wort for its strong and bitter taste. Depending on where you live, you may call *Glechoma hederacea* either creeping Charlie, ground ivy, or runaway robin because of its aggressive runners. Cat's foot is named for the shape of its leaves, ale hoof because it was commonly used in the making of beer and ale, and field balm because it has been used for as a general heal-all herb for balms, salves, and teas for thousands of years.

So next time you want a hearty cup of coffee, make sure you add a pinch or two of beard of monk (chicory). For a nice calming cup of tea, try some blood of Hestia (chamomile), both of which would be delicious with a yummy piece of scaldhead (brambleberry) pie.

Create and Work with an Energy Ball

With the advent of modern technology, we can talk to loved ones all over the world with barely more effort than the wave of a hand. Sometimes, though, even with the ability to communicate, the physical distance between us might make us feel helpless, especially if our friends and family are in need. While we might not be able to be there for them in the flesh, we can help them metaphysically by working with energy balls. The energy ball is one of the most basic forms of outside energy manipulation. They are common and have a multitude of purposes. They have many names like Chi Ball, Psi Ball, Reiki Ball, and the list goes on. Some of their most common uses are for healing, protection, and spell casting. You can use them to literally send energy to someone or help someone in need. This particular energy ball is for distance healing and protection. How does it work? First, you need muster up your energy to create the ball itself.

Creating the Ball

The human body is surrounded by electromagnetic and electrostatic energy, often called an auric field. We can create energy quite easily. This is one of the ways to do so: Rub your hands together for a minute or two and notice that they get warm from the friction. To create an energy ball, once you feel that friction, cup your hands and very slowly pull them apart a few inches. Then just as slowly bring them a bit closer together. You will be able to feel the energy you've created in that space between your palms.

This is only one method of creating an energy ball. Other practitioners forego the rubbing of hands, and instead place their palms close together, facing each other, and then slowly move them apart and then together again. They continue doing this until they feel a slight resistance, which is an indication of energy.

In both methods, when you begin to feel the energy, mold this energy into the shape of a ball with your cupped hands, as if you're forming a ball of clay. As you're molding it, see this energy as a bright ball of light in your mind's eye. Now it's time to pick a color that matches your intentions.

Choosing the Appropriate Color for the Ball

Choose a color that fits the purpose of your energy ball, just as you would choose a candle color when practicing candle magick. For example, for love healing, you might select pink. For protection, you might select a deep indigo blue. Listen to your instincts and select the color that feels right to you.

Intention

Focus your goal into the ball. Envision the person you will be sending the ball out to and any specific area of the body that requires healing. You can also envision a general healing or protection. Keep in mind that healing is not just in the physical body. Some people might need a shot of confidence or help with grief or sorrow, or they might just need a feeling of well-being at times. Don't limit yourself to sending the ball to just the physical body.

Sending the Ball

I like to literally send the ball on its way, so when I've got the color and intention all set, I just push the energy ball away from my body and out of both my hands. (If it is meant for yourself, this is when you turn towards yourself and push it into your own body.) At the same time, in my mind's eye, I see it reaching the person it is intended for. If there is more than one area that needs healing, I see the ball split into as many balls as needed as it approaches the body, and they enter all the areas that need healing. Some people I know say that when the energy balls find their way in, they give off a more radiant light as if to let the sender know that all was successful. That's all there is to it. Creating, intending, and sending!

Mabon—September 19–22

Final Thoughts

Don't be discouraged if creating and sending an energy ball doesn't work for you right off the bat. Like everything else, it takes a bit of practice, but it gets easier and more successful each time. The old adage is correct: Practice makes perfect. Also remember that visualization and healing are best attempted when you are in a positive and relaxed frame of mind. Do healing only to those who are open to receiving it and who give their permission. And most importantly, any healing you send should not by any means be a substitute for professional medical care and advice.

Mabon Spells
The Magickal Apple

Apples ripen in the fall and consequently are featured heavily during harvest festivals, such as Mabon, the autumnal equinox. Welcome the fall with an apple spell.

You will need:

· An apple

· A knife

· A small cloth bag

Cut the apple in half widthwise. You will see that the seeds form a five-pointed star in the shape of a pentacle. Pluck the seeds out of the apple one by one and make a wish on each seed.

Place the seeds in a tiny cloth bag and put them on your altar or in a drawer for safekeeping. Take a bite of the apple then recite the following incantation:

Magickal fruit, please follow my lead,
And grant my desires of those things I need.
I ask that of thee with my best intention,
And I very much welcome your intervention.
So Mote It Be

Enjoy the rest of the apple. When your wishes start to come true, remove a seed for each wish, take it outdoors, and return it to nature.

A Nutty Prosperity Spell

Not having enough money can drive you nutty, but walnut is said to draw prosperity, so give this a try.

You will need:

- A walnut

- A green candle

- A small piece of paper

- A pen

Carefully crack the walnut in half and remove the fruit, then write the amount you need on the paper. Don't be greedy. Just ask for an amount that is needed.

Light the candle and let the wax drip into both sides of the walnut shells, making sure the edges are covered as well.

Place the paper inside the shells and seal them shut, then recite this incantation:

The amount written within this shell
Will be enough to do me well.
Please consent to my request,
And that will rid me of my stress.
So Mote It Be

Find a place to bury the shell where it won't be disturbed.

Cinnamon Abundance Spell

Cinnamon has many uses in magickal workings. It cleanses the sacral chakras and can inspire sensuality, natural healing, and prosperity. It's also good for warding off negativity and instills self-confidence. In this case, you will evoke the power to draw in money.

You will need:

- A green candle
- A small coin purse (or a small pouch)
- 4 shiny pennies
- A cinnamon stick (broken into pieces)

Light the candle and drop the cinnamon pieces into the coin purse. Hold the pennies in your hand and put your energy into them for a moment, then one by one, drop them into the purse or pouch and repeat the following incantation:

Shiny pennies, cinnamon bark,
This spell is done not on a lark.
I want to see my income grow.
My finances now are touch and go.
I must have money to get by
And wish you now to please comply
So Mote It Be

Blow out the candle and keep the purse or pouch close to you for a few days. Repeat the spell as often as is needed.

Autumn Leaves Wishes

The veil between worlds begins to thin during the period between Mabon and Samhain. When autumn leaves fall, use some of those fallen leaves to make your wishes come true.

You will need:

- As many leaves as you have wishes
- A marker or pen

Select a leaf for each wish and write your wish upon it.

Take the leaves to a nearby body of water, like a lake, river, pond, or beach, and drop the leaves into the water. Watch your wishes float away and repeat the following chant three times:

> Flowing water, send away
> All my wishes I ask for this day.
> So Mote It Be

Then walk away and don't look back.

Sometimes a little magick works wonders.

Keeping the House Spirits Happy

Many believe that every house has a spirit. If you believe that trees, bricks, or stones have a spirit or energy, it makes good sense that this spirit energy would be transferred into the home that was built with those materials. Give thanks and recognition to those who share your space and watch over you by leaving out offerings to them on a regular basis.

You will need:

- Pencil and paper
- Herbs or flowers from the garden, milk, honey, wine, beer, mead, fresh bread, or sweets

Set out a small bowl of what you are offering, in a place that won't be disturbed, indoors or out, then recite the following invocation:

> I feel your presence every day
> And honor you in this humble way.
> Even when there's much ado
> You make things right so I thank you.
> Through rain or shine, good times or bad, you persevere.
> Please accept my gratitude. I'm blessed that you're here.
> So Mote It Be

Place the incantation next to the bowl of offerings.

Pencils should be used rather than pens because graphite and wood come from the earth and graphite assists in chakra-alignment healing and encourages energetic flow.

Salt Protection

Salt is a powerful magickal tool. It's used in a variety of ways, such as grounding, healing, purification, blessings, in spell work, consecrations, and banishing, and as a powerful barrier that shields and protects because negative entities and energies cannot cross salt. So, if you feel the need for protection, it's time to grab a box of salt.

You will need:

· Enough salt to sprinkle around the perimeter of the place that needs protection.

It could be your home, your car, a particular room in your house, or wherever shielding is needed. (You can use your choice of sea salt, kosher salt, table salt, Himalayan pink salt, or black salt.)

Sprinkle the salt along the perimeters of your location of choice while reciting this incantation:

All negativity begone this day.
Whether energy or entity, you cannot stay.
Go back where you came from; you're not wanted here.
With this dusting of salt, you will now disappear.
So Mote It Be

Spill the Beans

Sometimes we know that someone isn't telling the truth. This spell will help you find out what you need to know.

You will need:

· A purple candle for wisdom and attunement

· A picture of the person who needs to tell the truth (or you can write their name on a piece of paper).

Put the picture or paper next to the candle, light the candle, and repeat the following incantation:

I cast this spell, this hour, this day,
To finally hear what you need to say.
You've kept your secret long enough.
It's time to come clean without any bluff.
By the power of three I conjure thee
To tell the truth unto me.
So Mote It Be

Blow out the candle and, if need be, repeat the spell once a day until you get the information you want.

Remember, the stronger your intent as you do the spell, the quicker your results will be.

House Entry Protection Spell

This spell is to keep unwanted spirits and negativity in general from getting through your door and into your house. Mabon is the perfect season to do home-protection spells, but this spell can be done any time you feel your humble abode needs a little extra protection.

You will need:

- A handful of sea salt

- A pinch of red or black pepper

- 3 mashed cloves of garlic

- A handful of rosemary

On the night of a full moon, use a mortar and pestle (or any other tool or appliance) to combine the ingredients and leave it on your windowsill overnight. The next morning, take the bowl outside and spread the contents around the outside of your front and back doors while repeating this incantation:

Essence of rosemary, garlic, pepper, and salt,
Please bring negativity to a sudden halt.

Mabon—September 19–22

Be it a spirit, danger, or curse,
It will hit the door and bounce back in reverse.
Nothing can enter without my consent,
Especially when it's got bad intent.
I banish you now; you're not wanted here.
This house will always remain free and clear.
So Mote It Be

To Protect Animals from Abuse

If there's one thing I despise it's cruelty to animals. All creatures should be treated with love and respect. Unfortunately, we can't be there to protect all the unfortunate animals at the hands of cruel and heartless humans, but we can take action against animal cruelty either in person or remotely with this magickal spell. Saint Francis of Assisi, who blesses pets, has his feast day on October 4th.

You will need:

- A purple candle

- A sharp pin

- Frankincense or patchouli incense

- A sprig of lavender

- A quartz crystal

Etch your intentions into the candle. It can be something in particular that you know about that must be stopped, or general. Light the incense and place the lavender next to the candle, then recite the following incantation:

Protect all abused creatures from violence and pain.
Protect them from those who are filled with disdain.
Protect them from hardship, anger, and greed.
Protect them from those who lie and mislead.
May karma take over with lightning speed

And stop the insanity; let those creatures be freed.
So Mote It Be

This spell is strongest when cast on the new moon.

Justice Candle Spell

Whether it be a legal matter or you've been judged wrongly in some other way, called upon Themis, the goddess of justice. Her symbol is the scales of justice, and she can help you get your problem resolved in a fair manner. This is the perfect spell for Libra season because Libras are represented by the scales.

You will need:

· A white candle

· A blue candle

· Frankincense

Put out your offerings, light the candles and incense, then repeat the following incantation:

Goddess of order, here is my plea,
I've been misjudged and need help from thee.
Day and night I've been feeling unnerved.
It's so important that justice be served.
With your assistance, things can turn around.
And put me back on solid ground.
So Mote it Be

Blow out the candles and watch the smoke carry your wishes up into the clouds.

Calm Down!

There are days when we are anxious, angry, nervous, worried, or just plain stressed out. This spell will get rid of that black cloud that's following you around and bring back the calm. Mabon is the perfect time for releasing.

Mabon—September 19–22

You will need:

- A yellow candle
- A fireproof bowl
- A fresh flower of any kind
- Pen with blue ink and a small piece of paper

Sit down and write out the top three things that are stressing you out, then put the paper in the fireproof bowl, light it, and repeat the following incantation as it burns:

Cleansing fire burning bright,
Help me turn what's wrong to right.
Get rid of stress, that's the enemy,
And now bring forth the needed serenity.
Let's clear the air to start anew,
And bring me the calmness I pursue.
So Mote It Be

After it has cooled down, place the flower in the bowl on top of the ashes and place the bowl where you can see it to remind you to stay calm.

Join Incenses to Boost Your Spells

Incense is used for clearing the air, for spell work, for aromatherapy, or just because you like the scent, but in all those cases, we usually burn only one scent at a time.

I keep all my incense together in a cupboard, and I noticed that when I opened the drawer, the aroma of all those blended scents was wonderful. That got me thinking that if we burn a specific scent, like rose for love, peace, and harmony, that a similar scent with some of the same properties might make the spell even stronger. I gave it a try and I felt as though it did give the spell an extra boost. See how it works for you.

You will need:

- Several sticks of incense of your choice

Light the incense together and recite the following incantation:

> Joined together, these blended scents
> Serve my desires and my intents.
> With pinch of that and a bit of this,
> The combinations cannot miss.
> As the smoke mingles, their strengths will unite,
> And the spell will grow stronger as it flies out of sight.
> So Mote It Be

To Keep a Spell from Backfiring

It's never a good idea to do spell work when you're under the weather or just not feeling up to par. Sometimes, though when need be, that spell still has to be cast.

If you're doubtful about whether you can be safe from backlash, use this binding spell to keep you out of harm's way.

You will need:

· A red ribbon

· Sandalwood or lavender incense

Light the incense and tie three knots in the ribbon, then repeat the following incantation:

> I tie these knots by the power of three,
> So no harm will bounce back to me.
> I send this spell to only one,
> And when received my work is done.
> So Mote It Be

Put the ribbon somewhere safe.

End Bad Luck

If you're having one of those weeks, months, or years when Murphy's Law kicks in and whatever can go wrong will go wrong, try this easy yet effective spell to help get rid of the bad luck.

Mabon—September 19–22

You will need:

- A green candle
- Small piece of paper and pen
- A heatproof bowl

Light the candle and think about all the bad luck you are experiencing and need to get rid of. Write it out on a piece of paper, then recite the following incantation:

> Enough, enough, I've had enough.
> Bad luck is making life too tough.
> With this paper I now burn,
> Bad luck will go and not return.
> So Mote It Be

Light the paper in the heatproof bowl, and let it burn to ash. As it burns, watch the bad luck go up in smoke. When the ashes cool, put them into a small food storage bag, seal the bag, and throw it into the garbage where it belongs.

Return the Favor

This is a multipurpose spell, created to give back what someone has wished upon you, whether good or bad. Whether they have taken the time to wish you glad tidings or a streak of bad luck, it's only polite to reciprocate. It's very important for you to know who the sender was before you cast the spell, because if it's aimed at the wrong person or the wrong reason, the spell will boomerang back on you.

You will need:

- A stick of an all-purpose incense like sandalwood or nag champa
- Pen and paper
- A fireproof bowl

Find a quiet spot, light the incense, and write the person's name and what you believe they have sent your way. Sit quietly for five minutes and think about that person and the wish that they bestowed on you, then light the piece of paper in the fireproof bowl and let it burn to ashes. Once the ashes have cooled, take the bowl outside and repeat this incantation:

Thanks for the wishes you've bestowed on me.
I'm sending them back in three times three.
For good or for bad, we reap what we sow.
And you will get yours, be my friend or foe.
So Mote It Be

Toss the ashes the ashes into the air and let the breeze carry them away.

Mabon Recipes
Heartwarming Baked Apples

4 Granny Smith apples or any other hard apple of your choice
4 tablespoons brown sugar or honey
½ teaspoon cinnamon
¼ cup raisins or to taste

Cut the apples in half horizontally and set the tops aside.

Core the apple bottoms and fill each with about a tablespoon of brown sugar and honey and one-fourth of the raisins, or to taste.

Place the tops back on the apples. Bake in a baking dish with a quarter inch of water in the bottom of the dish at 350 degrees until apples are soft and tender when pierced with a fork.

Magickally Marvelous Marinated Mushrooms

Mushrooms are so easy to cook with because they soak up flavor like a sponge. When you cook them slightly in a hot marinade, the flavor is immediately infused. Mushrooms also offer a whole host of health benefits and are rich in many essential nutrients. And if that weren't enough, in this recipe, there's enough garlic to keep those pesky vampires away.

1 pound fresh whole mushrooms
¼ cup vinegar

Mabon—September 19–22

¼ cup oil
6 cloves garlic, diced
1 teaspoon finely diced onion
¼ teaspoon dry mustard
salt and pepper to taste

Clean the mushrooms and set them aside.

Mix the remaining ingredients in a saucepan and bring to a boil, then reduce the heat and let them simmer for about five minutes. Add the mushrooms and cook briefly.

Conjuring Up a Honey Cake

A slice of this cake and a cup of tea will stimulate your senses, mind, body, and soul.

7 egg whites
7 egg yolks
1 cup sugar
1 cup honey
1 cup hot water
2 teaspoons coffee
2 teaspoons baking soda
4 cups flour

Whip the egg whites until firm and place them in the refrigerator until needed. Combine the yolks, sugar, and honey and mix on low speed until blended.

Mix the coffee with the hot water, and then mix with the sugar, yolks, and honey and stir.

Sift the baking soda into the flour, then slowly add the flour into the mixture, gently fold in the egg whites, and bake in a greased loaf pan at 375 degrees for about an hour.

Magickal Black Beans

Beans are magickal. After all, they made a wonder beanstalk for Jack. For us, they are a great source of protein, fiber, vitamins, and minerals, with low calories and low fat. Whip up a pot of these magickal black beans to reap the benefits. This recipe can easily be made vegan; simply leave out the bacon.

1 pound dried black beans
½ pound bacon
half a small onion, chopped
¼ cup cilantro, chopped
1 fresh jalapeño pepper
salt to taste

Cook the beans according to the directions on the package. Do not drain. Fry the bacon and crumble it into pieces.

Cut the jalapeño open and remove the seeds, but leave it intact.

Add the bacon, onion, jalapeño, cilantro, and salt to the beans. Simmer on low for about twenty-five minutes.

Remove from heat, place in a bowl, and cover.

Refrigerate and let it marinate for at least twenty-four hours before serving.

Saint Jan's Bewitching Banana Nut Tea Bread

Tea breads are a wonderful treat for a midday snack or anytime during the day or evening when you can sit back and relax. This recipe comes from Janet, the wife of radio host Ron Kolek. Now I know one of the reasons why Janet's husband has bestowed her sainthood title.

1¼ cups flour
2 teaspoons baking powder
¼ teaspoon baking soda
½ teaspoon salt
⅓ cup shortening (solid)
⅔ cup sugar
2 eggs
1 cup mashed bananas (two bananas)
1 teaspoon vanilla
optional: 1 cup walnuts

Mabon—September 19–22

Sift together flour, baking powder, baking soda, and salt.

Work shortening with a spoon until fluffy.

Gradually add sugar while continuing to work with a spoon until light.

Add eggs unbeaten one at a time, beating after each addition with a fork until fluffy.

Add nuts and beat well.

Stir in vanilla, add flour mixture alternately in thirds with bananas, and beat after each addition until smooth.

Turn into a greased loaf pan.

Bake in a preheated 350 degree oven for one hour and ten minutes.

Memories and the Wheel of the Year—An Exercise

So once again we've come to the end of one turn of the Wheel and the start of another. The Wheel of the Year spins far too quickly. The seasons change at such a rapid pace that one day it's May Day and in the blink of an eye, it's Samhain. So now what?

We all record meaningful moments in special ways. Some people keep journals, others have videos and photos of special occasions, and some just think back and remember their memories. Take a few moments of your time and write down your memories that coincide with each turn of the Wheel of the Year. I'm sharing mine with you as an example, and hopefully it will inspire you to do it for yourself.

Each season has its own charm and special meaning. Sometimes it's difficult to put those feelings into words, but way back around 1721, Italian composer Antonio Vivaldi was able to put it to music when he wrote four violin concertos, each of which gives musical expression to a season of the year. He fittingly called it *The Four Seasons*. It was a new idea in musical conception, and also among the first examples of program music, illustrating the world around the listener by musically emulating sounds of things like a spring cuckoo, flowing creeks, buzzing flies, frozen landscapes, and warm winter fires.

I'm not sure I can put my feelings about each season into words like Vivaldi did with music. To me, the four seasons of the year resonate most strongly as a feeling, rather than as a weather forecast. Each season possesses its own personality and characteristics, although these may vary depending on location. In Los Angeles, those weather changes are subtle rather than the dramatic seasons of many other areas, so for me, the strongest feelings I associate with each of the four seasons aren't tangible. They arrive with a lifetime of memories and emotions instead.

I could be wrong, but I think lots of people consider the season that coincides with their birthday their favorite. Those of us born during the summer not only have birthday memories, but also had the bonus of the three-month summer break from school, spending our days at the beach, or going away on summer vacation or to summer camp. For me, it was also time for a visit to Disneyland. Even though Disneyland was only about forty-five minutes away, we only went once a year, so it was a highly anticipated and wonderful day in the Magic Kingdom. So for me, summertime is largely about memories of childhood, but now, in my adult life, it is also a time to celebrate the summer solstice and Lughnasadh.

During the beginning of autumn, the weather here in southern California is still on the warm side, and the end of daylight saving time arrives stealing an hour of light in the evening. On the plus side, autumn is when the anticipation starts to build about the Halloween season, Samhain, and the autumnal equinox. While I have wonderful memories of dressing up, going trick-or-treating and, as I grew older, costume parties, Samhain, the witch's New Year, is also something I look forward to. It is a wonderfully magickal time in both my magickal and mundane worlds. We celebrate the cycle of death and rebirth. Samhain is a time to reflect on the past year, to reconnect with our ancestors, and to honor those who are no longer with us.

With winter comes the traditional holiday season, with all the bells and whistles. Winter is another very magickal time of the year with the winter solstice, Yule, and Imbolc. Childhood memories of Christmas past come flooding back. For me, it was big family gatherings for Christmas dinners, going to the Santa Claus Lane parade on Hollywood Boulevard

Mabon—September 19–22

each year, Christmas shopping, and looking at the holiday department store windows. The New Year is a time of new beginnings and making a fresh start. Imbolc, on February 1st, marks the coming of spring.

When I was a kid, spring was all about the Easter Bunny and Easter egg hunts, May Day, spring break, and, in elementary school, we danced around the maypole every year. We didn't have a clue as to why, but it was still a lot of fun. As I got older, spring also represented the fire festival of Beltane and the vernal equinox. Spring is a time of fertility, rebirth, and, for me, gardening. In southern California, there is no need to wait for the snow to melt or the ground to thaw. It's all about heading to a favorite nursery and stocking up on new seeds, new plants, and a whole new crop of goodness to come. Nothing makes me smile as much as walking outside and seeing all the bright colors of the flowers in bloom and the hummingbirds and butterflies zipping around from flower to flower.

And with that, the wheel comes full circle. As I mentioned at the beginning, the wheel seems to spin faster and faster each year. Although we can't slow it down, we can try to make the most of it as we live it. So when you have a spare few minutes, sit down and write down your memories and feelings for each season and then put them safely aside. No need to overthink it. The highlights (and maybe a lowlight or two) will pop into your head. Then a year from now, reread them and add new memories and feelings from this year. We can't turn back time, but we can remember and learn from it. Cherish the memories.

Some Famous Historical Witches

The world has always been filled with witches.

Witchcraft of some sort has probably existed since humans first walked the earth. Simple sorcery, such as setting out offerings to helpful spirits or using charms, can be found in almost all traditional societies. Prehistoric art depicts magickal rites to ensure successful hunting and seems to depict religious rituals involving people dancing in animal costumes.

Western beliefs about witchcraft grew largely out of the mythologies and folklore of ancient peoples, especially the Egyptians, Hebrews,

Greeks, and Romans. Witches in ancient Egypt purportedly used their wisdom and knowledge of amulets, spells, formulas, and figures to bend the cosmic powers to their purpose or that of their clients.

Biblical Witches

It's interesting to note that John the Baptist and Joan of Arc, both now significant Christian saints, were (and sometimes still are by some) considered to be witches. And they are not the only ones.

I suppose a good place to start when discussing the witches of the world would be with the Bible. Many consider the Bible not exactly witch-friendly, citing the passage "Thou shall not suffer a witch to live" found both in Deuteronomy and Exodus. However, this is a mistranslation of the original Hebrew that first appears in the King James Bible. King James was obsessed with witches, believing that they had tried to kill him and his queen. The original Hebrew verse and early Greek translations were more ambiguous regarding who should not be suffered to live. The Greek word translated as "witch" may also be translated as "poisoner" for example. So, is a poisoner not fit to live or a specific kind of poisoning witch? The phrase has been relentlessly analyzed for centuries.

Two of the most famous biblical witches are Jezebel and the so-called Witch of Endor (inspiration for the name Endora, the beloved character from the TV series, *Bewitched*).

Jezebel

Jezebel remains among the most famous witches.

The wife of King Ahab of Israel, she was the daughter of Ithobaal, King of Tyre, and a high priestess of the deities Baal and Asherah. Jezebel persuaded Ahab to encourage veneration of the Tyrian god Baal-Melkart, thus interfering with the exclusive worship of the Jewish god. The biblical Book of Kings describes how Jezebel was opposed by Elijah the Prophet. After Ahab's death, Jezebel's son became king of Israel, but Elijah encouraged a general to revolt. The son was killed, and Jezebel was thrown from a window to her death. Dogs consumed most of her body, fulfilling a prophecy that had been given by Elijah. In history and literature, she

Mabon—September 19–22

became the archetype of the wicked woman, a position she still retains in some circles.

The Witch of Endor

Then there was the witch of Endor from the Old Testament, perhaps more accurately known as the medium of Endor. Israel was then at war with the Philistines, whose army greatly outnumbered theirs. Saul, then king of Israel, was desperate for a solution and prayed to God, begging for a miracle to save his land. King Saul, however, had lost God's favor. Because of this, God ignored his call. King Saul sought to communicate with his deceased mentor, the prophet Samuel, as he believed Samuel would be able to advise him. King Saul ordered his servants to "Seek me a woman that hath a familiar spirit, that I may go to her, and inquire of her." His servant located a woman in Endor with the ability to consult with the dead—a medium—and King Saul went to see her—but in disguise. Saul requested that she call up the spirit of Samuel. She performed her magick and the spirit of Samuel appeared to her. Angry at being disturbed, Samuel tells the woman, who relays his message to Saul, that the Jewish army will be destroyed and that both he and his sons will be dead by tomorrow. The prophecy turns out to be true; the next day, the Philistines are victorious, Saul's sons have been killed in combat, and King Saul, badly injured, intentionally falls on his sword to kill himself. Everything the woman of Endor had told him had come to pass. She is shown to be accurate and not a fraud, and she behaves with kindness toward the doomed king, too.

Witches of the Burning Times

From a period that ranged from the 13th to the 18th centuries, depending upon location, witches or those accused of being witches were hunted relentlessly throughout Christian Europe and its colonies. Both religious and secular authorities participated in these witch hunts. Large masses of people—primarily women—were accused, arrested, interrogated, tortured, and often killed. Although most were anonymous, some victims were famous. Let's examine some of them.

200   *Magick for All Seasons*

Mother Shipton

Mother Shipton (c. 1488-1561) was a famous Yorkshire witch, prophet, and soothsayer, often called the English Nostradamus. According to legend, she was born in a cave outside of Knaresborough, North Yorkshire, during a violent thunderstorm. Her young mother was also considered to be a witch. The legend further states that the baby—the future Mother Shipton—was born hideously ugly, but what this means is not specified. It's now theorized that she may have had some sort of congenital anomaly. As she grew up, Mother Shipton demonstrated the gifts of prophecy, healing, and spellcasting. A number of her prophecies related to modern times have come true. Examples include her descriptions of inventions such as airplanes and cars, but Mother Shipton also made predictions relating to politics and war.

Elisabeth Sawyer

Elisabeth Sawyer, known as the "Witch of Edmonton," was accused of bewitching her neighbor's children and cattle ostensibly because her neighbors refused to buy brooms from her. Elizabeth was also accused of killing Agnes Ratcleif using magickal means. Her subsequent trial was among 17th-century England's most famous. She was questioned fiercely and her body searched for a so-called "witch's mark." Convicted by a jury, Sawyer was executed by hanging in 1621.

Margaret Jones

The first person to be executed for witchcraft in the Massachusetts Bay Colony, years before the Salem witch trials, Margaret Jones (1613—June 15, 1648) was a midwife, a profession often associated with accusations of witchcraft. A resident of Charlestown, now part of Boston, Margaret was indicted and found guilty of practicing witchcraft on June 15, 1648, based on accusations from patients and other midwives. She was also accused of having foreknowledge of things that others believed that she should not have known, as well as of having an imp.

Mabon—September 19–22

Isobel Gowdie

Among the most famous and mysterious witchcraft cases, Isobel Gowdie, born in approximately 1630, a Scottish farmer's wife, allegedly volunteered a confession of witchcraft to authorities in 1662. It is unknown why she confessed—or even if the confession was genuinely voluntary. Initially, she described shape-shifting into the form of a hare—an animal closely associated with witches in the British Isles—in which shape she visited the Queen of Elfhame (an archaic spelling of Elf Home, indicating Fairyland). The church authorities to whom she confessed were not interested in fairies; they wanted Isobel to discuss the devil—and eventually she did. Her confession is documented. However, everything after that is a mystery. We can only speculate as to what happened to Isobel.

Anne Boleyn

Anne Boleyn (c. 1500—May 19, 1536) was the second wife of England's King Henry VIII, following his divorce from his popular first wife, Catherine of Aragon. Henry's desire for this divorce was extremely controversial and forbidden by the Vatican. It caused Henry's break from the Church and his establishment of the Protestant Reformation. When Anne failed to deliver a male heir on Henry's time schedule, he began to regret this marriage (and desire another wife). Anne was accused of bewitching him into marriage. She was arrested, tried, and beheaded, demonstrating how charges of witchcraft were an extremely efficient way to get rid of inconvenient women.

Florence Newton

Compared to elsewhere in Europe, Ireland has had few witch trials; however Florence Newton (died 1661), known as the Witch of Youghal, was at the center of one of the most famous. Florence is described as an elderly beggar woman, which, like midwives, was a group often associated with witchcraft at the time. On March 24, 1661, Florence was arrested and jailed after various local people accused her of bewitching them and causing illness and other misfortune, and of murdering someone by using her witchcraft powers. She stood trial on September 11, 1661. Court documents have gone missing and so it is unknown what befell Florence. It is widely believed that she was convicted and executed, although a legend suggests that she died in jail before she could be killed.

Caroline of Brunswick

Caroline of Brunswick (1768-1821), wife of King George IV, was the Queen Consort of the United Kingdom of Great Britain and Ireland. It was not a happy marriage. King George agreed to marry her, as he was heavily in debt, and if he married an eligible princess, Parliament would increase his allowance. George was reputedly extremely drunk at their wedding. Husband and wife both detested each other, virtually from first sight. Their dislike of each other was no secret, and rumors spread that Caroline made wax effigies of the king, stuck needles in them, and threw them into the fire to torture him. Had those accusations been made two centuries earlier, no doubt Caroline would have been charged with witchcraft.

Mary Butters

The subject of another Irish witch trial, Mary Butters (c. 1770-c. 1850), known as the Carnmoney witch, was locally considered to be a wise woman, her specialty being the ability to lift curses from bewitched cattle and heal them. She was hired by a local farmer to lift such a curse that he perceived had been laid upon one of his cows. Reputedly, Mary *did* lift the curse but only one day later, the farmer, his wife, and son were discovered dead within their home, along with an injured Mary. She was charged with murder by magickal means in March 1850 and arrested. She claimed that a man, possibly the devil, carrying a bludgeon had come to the farm, killed the family, but only stunned her, knocking her unconscious. Mary apparently talked her way out of prison by claiming that she was needed to perform funerary rituals for the dead family, a claim that seems to have been accepted. Her story, unlike so many others, does not have an unhappy ending. Mary continued to live in the area for many years and apparently also continued her practice of unbewitching cattle.

Mabon—September 19–22

Fictional Witches

Before we get into real modern-day witches, this would be a good time to discuss those fictionalized baddies we see in the movies, on TV, and, yes, even in cartoons.

Broom Hilda

One of my favorite cartoon characters is Broom Hilda, a witch with green skin, a wart on the end of her nose, and long stringy hair. She wears a black dress, black shoes, striped stockings (one perpetually drooping), and a black hat with a daisy on top. According to the comic strip's official site, Broom Hilda is Attila the Hun's ex-wife. She is perpetually looking for a new husband, but due to her abrasive nature, the quest has thus far been unsuccessful. And then there's Witch Hazel of *Looney Toons* fame, who always left a trail of bobby pins behind her whether she was zooming off on her broom or throwing a fit.

Disney's Evil Witches

There were some animated witches who weren't quite as amusing, namely the Disney witches. There are thirteen of them all together. From Maleficent in *Sleeping Beauty* to *Snow White's* evil queen to Ursula, the sea witch of *The Little Mermaid*, these witches have scared generations of children.

Wicked Witch of the West and Others

Speaking of scary witches, the Wicked Witch of the West comes to mind, as does Anjelica Huston's portrayal of The Grand High Witch in the movie *The Witches*, which, despite depicting witches as having scabby heads, evil tempers, and clubbed feet, is a favorite movie, as is *The Witches of Eastwick*. Those three are more down-to-earth, despite their carousing with the devilish character played by Jack Nicholson. One of the scariest witches in the movies is Mortianna, who is the sheriff of Nottingham's mother in *Robin Hood: Prince of Thieves*. She's hard to look at, rather disgusting, and evil to the core.

Beautiful Witches

But movies don't always stick to depictions of witches as hideous. Beautiful witches include Veronica Lake in the 1942 movie, *I Married a Witch*, Glinda the Good Witch in *The Wizard of Oz*, and Kim Novak in *Bell, Book, and Candle*, to name but a few. Many of the witches and wizards in the *Harry Potter* movies serve as positive role models. And, for the most part, Samantha, Endora, Aunt Clara, and Uncle Arthur from the *Bewitched* TV series look like "regular" people, as does the titular Sabrina of *Sabrina the Teenage Witch*, and the cast of *Charmed*.

In fact, the only time you see real witches on TV looking like the "stereotypical witches" one might expect is around Halloween when those "Let's talk to a witch on Halloween" segments show up. That's when the media bends over backwards to find witches who are very, uh, "colorful," shall we say? They always seem a little overdramatic and sometimes a bit off. But then again, the powers that be seem to think that viewers would be bored to tears by a "normal-looking, normal-acting" witch. It's a shame that the stereotype has stuck and is exploited at the drop of a hat, but unfortunately, I don't think that's going to change anytime soon.

Modern-Day Witches

There are, however, a lot of us out there who are not only well-respected by other witches, but in the mainstream as well.

Raymond Buckland

A significant figure in the history of Wicca, Raymond Buckland (1934-2017) was a High Priest in both the Gardnerian and Seax traditions. He was the first person in the United States to openly admit to being a practitioner of Wicca. He introduced the lineage of Gardnerian Wicca to the United States in 1964, after having been initiated by Gardner's High Priestess Monique Wilson in Britain the previous year. Buckland later formed his own tradition dubbed Seax-Wica, which derives from Anglo-Saxon Paganism. His book *Buckland's Complete Book of Witchcraft*, first published in 1986, remains a classic.

Mabon—September 19–22

Gerald Gardner

Gerald Brosseau Gardner (1884-1964) is the father of modern Wicca. Born near Liverpool, England, Gardner spent much of his life traveling—he was involved in the tea industry in Ceylon, spent time in the jungles of Borneo, and was employed by the government in Malaya. Gardner studied magickal customs, folklore, and local mysticism wherever he went. A leading authority on antique knives and their use in witchcraft, his first book, *Keris and Other Malay Weapons* (1936), is considered the authoritative work on Malay and Indonesian magickal knives.

Gardner retired in 1936 and returned to England, where he became involved with local witchcraft practices. He began his own coven in 1947. Gardnerian Wicca, the oldest and most formal of modern Wiccan traditions, is based on his teachings. Gardner coauthored *The Gardnerian Book of Shadows* with High Priestess Doreen Valiente.

Sybil Leek

Then there are some from years ago, like Sybil Leek (1917-1982), who weren't shunned for being witches and were both accepted and respected. Sybil was Britain's most famous witch and rose to media fame in the 1950s after the repeal of the 1735 Witchcraft Act of 1951. She had a great impact on the formation of neo-Pagan witchcraft. When Sybil came to America, she was contacted by Hans Holzer, widely considered to be the father of parapsychology, who invited her to join him investigating hauntings and psychic phenomena. Sybil made frequent appearances on television and may be the first "celebrity witch." An astrologer and diviner, Sybil Leek was also an extremely prolific author.

Aleister Crowley (1875-1947)

Aleister Crowley, an English occultist, magus, mystic, prolific author, and mountaineer, exerted a profound influence on modern witchcraft that continues today. He is the founder of the religion Thelema. A controversial figure, Crowley was widely known in his lifetime as "the wickedest man in the world." He savored his reputation.

In 2002, a BBC poll described him as being the seventy-third greatest Briton of all time. References to him can be found in the works of numerous writers, musicians, and filmmakers, and he has also been cited as a key influence on many later esoteric groups and individuals, including Kenneth Anger, Gerald Gardner, Timothy Leary, and Jimmy Page.

Laurie Cabot

Laurie Cabot was born March 6, 1933. A High Priestess, author, and civil rights activist, Cabot was a trailblazer in American witchcraft. She is the founder of the Cabot Tradition of Witchcraft, which focuses on witchcraft as both a science and a religion, as well as on psychic development. In 1971, she opened the first witchcraft shop in Salem, Massachusetts, which quickly became a popular tourist destination. Michael Dukakis, then Governor of Massachusetts, dubbed Laurie the official witch of Salem in 1977. Laurie Cabot founded the Witches' League for Public Awareness and the Project Witches' Protection, organizations dedicated to preventing discrimination against witches and to combatting misinformation and the stereotypes that have long plagued witches and witchcraft.

Laurie Cabot's Book of Shadows, written by Laurie Cabot with Penny Cabot and Christopher Penczak, details the lore, rituals, and history of the Cabot Tradition.

Everyday Witches

For every one witch you see on TV or read about in the newspaper, there are more of us than you can imagine behind the scenes, doing good work. If you're reading this book, you might be one of them.

So there you have it. A brief tale of witches throughout history and just the tip of the iceberg.

There have always been and will always be witches. From biblical times to the Burning Times and continuing today, witches are very much alive in our world. The belief in and the practice of magick have been present since the earliest human cultures and continue to have an important role in many cultures today. The concept of witchcraft as harmful or

Mabon—September 19–22

malevolent is often treated as a cultural ideology, providing a scapegoat for human misfortune. This was particularly the case in early modern Europe, eventually leading to large-scale witch hunts. These were devastating, resulting in the deaths of many innocent people.

Even in our supposedly enlightened society, witch hunts continue to this day, with tragic consequences. There are instances of lynching reported with some regularity from much of sub-Saharan Africa, rural northern India, the Middle East, and Papua New Guinea. There are also some countries where practicing witchcraft is illegal.

Nonetheless, those called to witchcraft soldier on, in hopes that our society will continue toward the way of acceptance and light. The world needs witches as much as it needs any other kind of human. The path of the witch is a loving one, so continue to brew your potions, continue to cast your spells, and continue to celebrate the Wheel of the Year.

APPENDIX

A Glossary of Witchcraft Terminology, Crystals, and Candles

Witchcraft Terminology

Alchemy—A chemical science and philosophy focused on the transmutation and transformation of base metals into gold through the use of the mythical philosopher's stone. Alchemy gained popularity in Europe during the Middle Ages and the Renaissance, and is often thought of as a precursor to modern chemistry.

Altar—An altar is usually some kind of sacred work space, often on a table or shelf, for devotional, spiritual, or ritual work. Often an alter is adorned with candles, offerings, incense, or other magickal tools and practices. Alters can be specific to a particular practice, like ancestor or deity veneration, or for general witchcraft.

Aspect—When referring to a deity or entity, an aspect is an archetype, form, facet, or persona of that deity or entity. In astrology, the term "aspect" refers to an angle that planets make with each other in a natal chart.

Astral—The multidimensional, nonphysical plane known as the "astral realm," which can be visited through astral projection.

Athame—A ceremonial double-edged knife used in ritual magick and Wiccan practices. The athame usually has a black handle and is associated with the elements of fire and air.

Balefire—An open fire used in a ritual or spell.

Banish—The magickal act of repelling something or someone from a person or place.

Besom—A magickal broom used in cleansing rituals, besoms are also used to invite positive energies to a space, often a home.

Book of Shadows—A Book of Shadows is a personal magickal tome written by an individual practitioner. In addition to spells, a Book of Shadows may contain rituals, observations, recipes, and personal wisdom. In some witchcraft traditions, the Book of Shadows is a book of traditions and spells that is passed down from teacher to student. The Book of Shadows is traditionally written and copied by hand.

Burning Times—This is a name given to the witch hunts and witchcraft trials in Europe and its colonies, roughly between 1350 and 1750 CE.

Charge—In witchcraft and magick, to "charge" an item, person, or space is to intentionally fill it with a practitioner's energy.

Charm—From the Latin *carmen*, meaning "song" or "incantation." The word is a term for both magick and for small trinkets that protect their owner from evil.

Circle—In magickal traditions, a circle may refer to a magick circle, or to a gathering of Pagans or witches for a ritual.

Coven—A group of witches is called a coven, like a group of bats is a cauldron or a group of ravens is an unkindness. Some covens are very formal in structure, depending on tradition, while others are more familial.

The Craft—"The Craft" refers to the practice of witchcraft as a whole (and not the movie of the same name).

Elementals—The personified spirits of each element, such as gnomes for earth, undines for water, sylphs for air, and salamanders for fire.

Magick for All Seasons

Equinox—Equinoxes happen twice a year, once in the spring (around March 21st) and once in the fall (around September 21st), when the durations of night and day are equal.

Esoteric—Magickal practices designed for a small initiated group or practices requiring restricted or otherwise arcane knowledge are esoteric in nature. The word derives from the ancient Greek *esôterikós*, meaning "belonging to an inner circle."

Evil Eye—Also known as the *nazar, ayin hara, malocchio,* and *mal de ojo.* It is a common belief in many cultures that a look or stare potentially brings bad luck for the person at whom it is directed. The cause may be rooted in envy or dislike, but the evil eye can be cast completely involuntarily.

Full and New Moons—The different phases of the moon's cycle are significant in some Pagan traditions, especially in Wicca, where the moon is associated with the goddess. Wiccans believe the inherent spiritual power in nature is greatest on the night of the full moon. They gather at that time to work magick related to increase, fullness, and fruition, such as prosperity or growth. On new moons, Wiccans often gather for ritual that relates to the unseen, or for goals that may need a period of gestation.

Grimoire—A book of magick spells and rituals.

Handfasting—A ritual in which the hands of a couple are bound together, whether literally or symbolically. It represents a commitment to each other and often takes place during a marriage ceremony. The word may be used as a synonym for "marriage" and often serves as the modern Wiccan or Pagan sacrament of marriage.

Hex—A hex is a curse or spell cast with nefarious intent. The word derives from the German *hexen,* which references witchcraft. In modern German, a *hexe* is a witch.

A Glossary of Witchcraft Terminology, Crystals, and Candles

Incantation—A spoken spell or charm, which may be expressed in chanting or song. The crucial component that defines an incantation is its words. Feel free to experiment with your own magick words.

Magick—Some practitioners spells this word with a *k* and some spell it the way it's seen more often in the nonmagical community—"magic." Typically those who spell the word with the *k* do so to distinguish the practice of magick from stage magic or illusionism. The practice was promoted by Aleister Crowley. Use whichever feels right to you and your practice.

Pagan—The term "Pagan" derives from the Latin *paganus*, which originally indicated a "country dweller" or a "rustic." In the early days of Christianity, the new religion was embraced by the Roman military and urban dwellers. Those dwelling in the countryside—the Pagans—were, however, resistant. Eventually, the term became a synonym for "not-Christians" or those who clung to ancient polytheistic religious traditions. The term is now used to refer to modern people with similar spiritual orientations. Numerous Pagan and neo-Pagan traditions now exist. For many Pagans, the term suggests a life lived close to the land. Nature-based spirituality is an important concept in contemporary Paganism. Some Pagans focus on reviving polytheistic systems of belief and practice. Still others embrace Paganism as a religion that offers feminine and queer concepts related to divinity.

Pendulum— A divinatory tool that is hung from a separate tool or hand that gives yes or no answers based on the direction it swings when asked a question.

Pentagram—A five-pointed star that serves as popular symbol in witchcraft and Paganism. It may be worn as a religious symbol in the way that Christians wear a cross. It serves as an amulet of protection and may symbolize the elements.

Quarters—The four corners that are associated with the cardinal directions in a magickal circle. They serve as symbolic guards when called upon during a magick ritual. They are also associated with the four elements.

Runes—An ancient alphabet that uses symbols to represent aspects of life, nature, and spirituality. They are carved into small stones or sticks and are often used in divination. They originated in Scandinavia around 2,000 years ago.

Sabbat—Each of the eight Wiccan holidays in the Wheel of the Year, starting with the witch's New Year, Samhain, and continuing with Yule, Imbolc, Ostara, Beltane, Litha, Lammas/Lughnasadh, and Mabon. Each corresponds with a natural cycle of the earth, like the equinoxes and solstices. They are often celebrated with good company and rituals.

Scrying—An ancient form of divination which involves gazing into a surface such as a crystal ball, mirror, water, or flames.

Shadow Work—This is a practice of introspection where the practitioner examines the deep and repressed aspects of the personality. Shadow work is difficult but rewarding.

Sigil—Often used in high magick, sigils are symbols, seals, or glyphs that are charged.

Solstice—The shortest and longest days of the year, usually around June 21 and December 21. They are highly magickal days, associated with midsummer and midwinter, respectively.

So Mote It Be—A common way of ending a spell or ritual. It means "So must it be." You'll notice I like to close most of my spells this way.

Wiccan Rede—The word "rede" derives from Middle English, meaning "advice" or "rule." The Wiccan rede provides the key moral system for Wiccans; the rede says, "If it harm none, do what thou will."

A Glossary of Witchcraft Terminology, Crystals, and Candles

Crystals

Agate—This crystal is typically red, brown, and orange, but it can come in a whole spectrum of colors. Used for balancing, grounding, protection, and emotional healing, agate has been a popular crystal since it was used in ancient Rome. It can be found all over the world, from the United States to Brazil to Morocco.

Alexandrite—Raw alexandrite is a greenish color, but when polished or used in jewelry, it can take on a reddish or purplish color. Found on four continents, this crystal promotes balance and harmony, and it can help with sense of self and willpower.

Amazonite—Amazonite is a strong filter, both filtering information received by the brain, allowing the user to look at a situation objectively, and filtering electromagnetic emanations. As a filter, it is a great stone for health. It's found in North America, South America, Europe, Asia, and Africa.

Amber—Not actually a crystal, but fossilized resin from trees, amber is associated with warmth, grounding, and healing. It is primarily used for health, both physical and mental. Known for healing pain, amber is found in Europe, but it has also been found in the Dominican Republic and Myanmar.

Amethyst—One of the most versatile crystals, amethyst provides psychic protection, improved health, enhanced magickal practices (including divination, astral projection, spell work, etc.), and strengthened relationships, both romantic and platonic. It is associated with the third eye and crown chakra and is found all over the world. Classic amethyst is purple with clusters of small prismatic columns, but amethyst has many forms.

Aquamarine—Aquamarine is a beautiful turquoise color and has traditionally been associated with the sea. Mostly used for its strong calming properties, it is often used for meditation, as it invokes a higher state of consciousness. It's also a great stone for emotional healing and a greater understanding of oneself and others. Aquamarine is found on all continents except Australia and Antarctica.

Aventurine—Known as a lucky and positive green stone, aventurine is stabilizing and protective. It is found in Brazil, Italy, India, Russia, Tibet, and Nepal.

Azurite—Found in Australia, South America, Europe, and Africa, azurite is great for psychic powers, divination, and inner vision. Used in ancient Egypt, this crystal can open your mind and change your worldview. Azurite is a deep blueish purple, sometimes with traces of green.

Beryl—This crystal eases stress and anxiety. A favorite of ancient Greece, this stone also has a place in history in England, as Dr. Dee's crystal ball was made of beryl. It is also great for emotional baggage and protection against manipulation. Typically a yellow-gold, beryl can be found in North America, South America, Europe, Asia, and Australia.

Black tourmaline—Black tourmaline shares all the characteristics of regular tourmaline, but it is even more protective, neutralizing threats like curses or psychic attacks. It is useful against any negative energy, including electromagnetic disturbances.

Bloodstone—This dark-green stone is often interspersed with bit of red. Primarily found in Australia, Brazil, China, Russia, India, and the Czech Republic, the ancient Babylonians thought bloodstone held magickal properties. Today, bloodstone is great for health, including boosting the immune system, and grounding and protection.

Carnelian—Beloved by the ancient Egyptians, this stone helps the user make good choices and helps with self-trust and love. It also eases the fear of death. Usually a dark orange, it can be found on every continent except Antarctica.

A Glossary of Witchcraft Terminology, Crystals, and Candles

Cat's eye—Associated with heightened intuition, cat's eye is also said to protect the aura and help with grounding. This brown crystal is found almost everywhere.

Chrysolite—This stone is more commonly known as peridot.

Citrine—Citrine is linked with the sun, due to its bright yellow to orange coloring and associations with positivity. It transforms and grounds negative energy and is known to smooth over issues in groups. It's found in the United States, Brazil, France, Russia, Madagascar, and the UK.

Clear quartz—Widely acknowledged as one of the most versatile and well-known crystals, quartz has been used for millennia by many ancient civilizations. Clear crystal is a highly effective healer and energizer. It can be found all around the globe.

Diamond—Symbolizing wealth and love, this famous stone is the hardest known natural substance. Some ancient civilizations claimed it was such an effective healer that it could counteract poisons. It is found in North America, South America, Africa, Asia, and Australia.

Emerald—Emerald is said to boost fertility and love, and promote health. The first use is thought to have been around 5,000 years ago. In antiquity, it was thought to protect against magicians and malevolent magick. It's found in South America, Africa, Asia, and eastern Europe.

Fluorite—This well-known stone can be pink, blue, yellow, or—its most famous form—purple and green. Fluorite helps with organization, providing a strong tool for structure and order. A generally positive crystal, it wards off negativity and stress and brings grounding and intuition. It's found in North America, South America, Europe, Australia, and Asia.

Garnet—This versatile stone is deep red in color. It is a strong protector, but not just passively; it reverses the harm onto those who wished or cast it. Garnet is highly associated with love, passion, devotion, and sex. It's found in the southwestern United States, Europe, South Africa, and Australia.

Green aventurine—Green aventurine holds all the powers of aventurine, but it is also a wonderful harmonizer. This comforting stone has wonderful healing properties. It can be found in South America, Europe, and Asia.

Green calcite—Calcite is an amplifier of psychic and metaphysical abilities, and green calcite is known to bring abundance and fertility. The stone also moves stagnant energy and can be found in North America, South America, and Europe.

Green jasper—Found worldwide, green jasper shares all the properties of jasper. Additionally, it can cure obsessions and help balance priorities.

Hyacinth—This is another name for brown zircon.

Jade—Jade helps with stability and protection. This nurturing stone can be found in the United States, China, Italy, Myanmar, Russia, and parts of the Middle East. Its color is a beautiful green; its name has become synonymous with that specific shade.

Jasper—A great absorber of negative energy, this crystal is known as a wonderful nurturer. Jasper comes in many forms and colors, all with slightly different strengths. The original jasper, however, is red or dark orange. It is found worldwide.

Lace agate—Lace agate shares all the characteristics of agate. However, lace agate is more spiritually attuned than the traditional stone and gently encourages sensitivity and confidence. Beautifully striated and typically light blue, this crystal is found in the United States, Brazil, India, Africa, and the Czech Republic.

Lapis lazuli—Lapis lazuli is a versatile and powerful stone. A deep blue, this stone is excellent for psychic work and maximizes spiritual power. Also associated with love, it comes from Russia, Chile, the US, Italy, and parts of the Middle East.

Lodestone—Naturally magnetic, lodestone is used in meditation and is typically a slate gray. It can be found everywhere in the world except Africa, Asia, and Antarctica.

A Glossary of Witchcraft Terminology, Crystals, and Candles   217

Moonstone—This crystal has gentle, feminine energy. More powerful during a waxing moon, this stone enhances clairvoyance and tempers emotion. It can open the mind and is associated with the goddess. Lightly striated, this stone in found in India, Sri Lanka, and Australia.

Obsidian—Used by the ancient civilizations of what is now Mexico, obsidian is known to be blunt in what is reveals; it will show flaws and weaknesses. That said, it will not hold back in healing either. Good for scrying, this traditionally black stone comes from the volcanic regions of Mexico.

Onyx—This stone offers defense against negative energies, like the evil eye. Found in the Americas, parts of Europe, and South Africa, onyx gives strength and is helpful in relationships, whether they need to be stronger or let go. It is usually shiny and black but can have other color in it as well.

Opal—Great for psychic connections, this beautiful crystal comes in many different colors. Found on most continents, opal is traditionally said to provide stealth when needed. It is also associated with matters of the heart and emotions.

Orange carnelian—Along with the properties of carnelian, orange carnelian balances emotions and helps the user overcome fear.

Pearl—Not actually a crystal, pearl is formed inside an oyster around a grain of sand or other small object. White and iridescent, natural pearls are rare but in recent years, man-made pearls have become more common. They promote healing, protection, positivity, and balance.

Peridot—A highly protective stone, peridot is green and found in North America, South America, Europe, Africa, and the Middle East. It is known to purify the body and mind and to provide guidance in times of need.

Quartz—A highly versatile stone, quartz has tens of variations. The stone increases and elevates all forms of magick. It protects, energizes, cleanses, and attunes to the user. Since it has so many uses, it can often be substituted for other crystals. It's found everywhere.

Rhodonite—This stone is sensitive, providing nurturing to old emotional wounds and providing healing and forgiveness. Usually pink with some black, this stone is found in Spain, Germany, Sweden, Russia, Mexico, and Brazil.

Rose quartz—Rose quartz is a romantic stone; some say it is the most important crystal for love. It will attract relationships, as well as heal them. Emotional healing, increased empathy, and self-love are also amplified by this stone. It is found in the United States, Brazil, Germany, South Africa, Madagascar, India, and Japan.

Ruby—Famous for its deep-red color and popularity in jewelry, it's also known for its associations with passion and love—both for partners and for life. It is said to warn the user by darkening when danger is near. Also a stone of abundance, ruby is found in Central America, India, Russia, and many parts of Africa.

Sapphire—Sapphire is known for its beautiful blue, but it can also come in many other colors. It calms and focuses the mind and offers wisdom to the user. Popular in jewelry, sapphire is found on all continents except Antarctica.

Sardonyx—Black, orange, brown, and red, sardonyx is found in Brazil, Russia, Turkey, the Middle East, and India. It provides strength, protection, high morals, happiness, and luck.

Smoky quartz—A grounding and cleansing crystal, this is one of the many forms of quartz. It's associated with the earth and aids with keeping realistic and positive. It is found worldwide.

A Glossary of Witchcraft Terminology, Crystals, and Candles

Snowflake obsidian—This form of obsidian shares all the characteristics of the original form, but specializes in purity and balance. It's a calming stone, good for unblocking emotions. It is also found in the volcanic regions of Mexico.

Sunstone—Sunstone brings joy and happiness. With a strong solar energy, this crystal can bring fortune and luck, as well as repel unsavory people. It puts a positive spin on life and is found in Canada, the United States, Norway, Greece, and India.

Tanzanite—Purple and blue, this stone is a form of zoisite. Strongly associated with emotional balance and higher consciousness, tanzanite can also be helpful for burnout and overwork. This form is only found in Tanzania.

Tiger's eye—Tiger's eye corresponds with luck, prosperity, and self-confidence. It also helps unlock creativity. Its name is derived from its striated dark-brown and gold-orange color. It is found in United States, Mexico, India, Australia, and South Africa.

Topaz—Topaz comes in many different forms. A happy and positive stone, it's typically energizing, but the individual forms' associations range from psychic clearing to self-confidence. Some forms are only found in certain locations, but as a group they can be found worldwide.

Tourmaline—Known for encouraging plants to grow, tourmaline also takes heavy, dense energy and changes it into a lighter vibration. Grounding and highly protective, it also is used for deep self-reflection and scrying. It is found on every continent except Antarctica.

Turquoise—Found in most places other than Asia, turquoise corresponds with good fortune, balancing between heaven and earth, and elevating the spiritual self. Also providing protection, it's found North America, South America, Europe, Asia, and the Middle East.

Yellow agate—Associated with joy and happiness, this stone also helps with focus and clarity.

Yellow topaz—Increases positivity, faith, and friendship. Yellow topaz is also associated with the sun, warmth, and self-expression.

Zircon—Zircon is said to help lovers connect and protect the physical body. It also clears the mind and filters thoughts. It can be green, blue, gold, clear, or red. It's found in Australia, the United States, Sri Lanka, and Canada.

Candle Color Symbolisms

Red—Red candles are used for grounding energy, strength, passion, courage, lust, charisma, fire element, bravery, and confidence. The color red is also associated with the root chakra.

Orange—Creativity, success, justice, opportunity, ambition, cultivating energy, passion, confidence, and warmth are associated with orange candles.

Yellow—You can use yellow candles for intelligence, focus, confidence, inspiration, pleasure, happiness, memory, joy, and wealth. Yellow is connected to the sun, so use this color when you need a boost of solar power.

Green—Green is associated with all things nature. It's also great for healing, money, financial matters, love, fertility, growth, abundance, manifestation, and plant magick.

Blue—Light-blue candles are great for communication, calm, and harmony, while dark blue is good for intuition and introspection, as well as psychic endeavors, like astral projection. Blue is also related to the throat chakra.

Purple—Being a color traditionally associated with royalty, purple candles are used for asserting influence, enhancing psychic abilities, establishing authority, wisdom, knowledge, spiritual power, and independence.

A Glossary of Witchcraft Terminology, Crystals, and Candles

Brown—Home, protection, animals, stability, family, and working with the earth are associated with brown candles.

Black—Black candles are used for banishing negativity, protection, grounding, binding, transmutation, establishing or reestablishing boundaries, and protecting your energy.

Pink—Pink candles deal with the softer side of love, like nurturing, emotional healing, and self-care and self-love.

Gold—Solar energy and cultivating health, wealth, and good fortune are the properties of gold candles.

White—White candles are versatile and can be substituted for candles of any other color. They are connected to spirituality, peace, the higher self, purity, truth, aura balancing, and cleansing the chakras.

Indigo—Associated with the higher self, indigo candles open the third eye, and aid in psychic development, intuition, divination, and meditation.

Silver—Silver candles have a soft, feminine energy and are therefore linked with the moon, dreams, meditation, and messages in your dreams.

RECOMMENDED READING

Botanicals

Blackthorn's Botanical Magic by Amy Blackthorn (Weiser Books, 2018)

The Witching Herbs by Harold Roth (Weiser Books, 2017)

Crystals

Crystal Basics by Nicholas Pearson (Destiny Books, 2020)

The Encyclopedia of Crystals by Judy Hall (Fair Winds, 2013)

Incense

The Big Book of Magical Incense by Sara Mastros (Weiser Books, 2021)

The Complete Incense Book by Susanne Fischer-Rizzi (Sterling, 1998)

GUIDE TO PRACTICES, SPELLS, AND RECIPES

Samhain

Practices and Tips

The Ancient Art of Scrying by Tim Shaw   17

Building an Ancestor Altar   4

Cartomancy   12

Divination   8

Great-Grandma Sophie's Witchy Tips   3

Spirit Guides   6

Samhain Spells

Ancestor Offerings   22

Birthday Blessing   34

Birthday Blessing Candle Spell   35

Creating an Ancestor Candle   33

Enchant Your Jewelry   31

Honor and Remember Candle Spell   28

Jack-O'-Lantern Spell   24

The Mirror of Perception   30

New Wand Blessing   27

Ring the Ancestor Bell   23

Samhain Renewal   25

Spirit Guide Invocation   26

Tarot Motivation   30

Thanksgiving Spell of Appreciation   29

Thirteen Wishes for Friday the 13th   24

Transform a Necklace into a Pendulum   32

Voyager's Prayer for a Cherished Pet   28

Samhain Recipes

Garlic-Onion Relish   38

Samhain Potato Casserole   36

Spellbinding Sweet-and-Sour Cabbage Soup   37

Yule

Practices and Tips

Birthday Stones   44

Birthstones   40

Yule Spells

Air Travel Protection   45

Cinnamon Stick Candles   47

Cleansing Your Aura   46

Clearing the Air in the Workspace   48

Get Well Healing Spell   53

Holiday Protection   46

Leave the Year Behind   53

Relax! The Holidays Are Over   54

Relieve Depression   52

Shut Up!   49

Sleep through the Night Meditation   49

Throw the Snow!   51

Warding Off the Evil Eye   50

Wish upon a Pinecone   44

Yule Recipes

Buttered Beer   58

Chestnut Soup   58

Fiendishly Good Black-Eyed Pea Salad   56

Ginger Wine   57

Mincemeat Pies   59

Plum Pudding   62

Stuffed Dates in Honey   62

Sugar Plums   65

Wassail   55

Imbolc

Practices and Tips

Creating Your Own Magick Spells   71

Make an Ice Candle   70

Plant Spirits in the Garden   68

Imbolc Spells

Besom Blessing   74

Cleanse Your House with Sound   76

An Easy Binding Spell   78

Goodbye and Good Riddance Spell   80

Just Walk Away Spell   79

Lucky Saint Patrick's Day Candle Spell   77

New Beginnings   72

Refreshing Your Home   73

Reverse the Hex   78

Guide to Practices, Spells, and Recipes   227

The Sky's the Limit Banishing Spell   73

Sweep Negativity Away   74

Torch Your Troubles   81

Unwanted Energy Cleanse   76

Imbolc Recipes

Crepes to Charm   82

Dragon-Eye Breakfast Sandwich   84

Rosemary Salt   82

Sweet Spirit Angel Delight   83

Ostara

Practices and Tips

Creating and Working with Witch Bells   88

Plant a Witch's Moon Garden   91

The Three Cs—Cleansing, Consecrating, and Charging Your Tools   90

Ostara Spells

Butterfly Wish   96

Easter Egg Magick   94

Energizing Eggshell Powder   95

Healing Candle Spell   104

Holy Week Manifestation   97

Job Interview Spell   97

Moon Water   105

Mother Earth Protection Spell   98

New Pet Blessing   104

Plant an Egg Abundance Spell   99

Plant Your Crystals   100

Seed Magick   93

Spring Cleaning   101
A Thousand Wishes   102
To Find What's Lost   103

Ostara Recipes
Dilly Pink Pickled Eggs   109
Magickal Properties of Fruit in Cooking   108
Magickal Properties of Herbs and Botanicals   107

Beltane

Practices and Tips
Elementals   112
Never Step into a Fairy Ring   113

Beltane Spells
Beltane/May Day Magickal Wishing Tree   115
Garden Spirits Blessing with Sun Water   116
Grounding Spell   117
Happy Aquarium Spell   123
Knot Your Troubles Away   118
Making a May Basket   116
Pet Protection Bell   121
Return to Your Source   120
Sachet of Protection   124
Saint Anthony Spell: Tony, Tony   123
Seven-Day Memorial Altar Spell   122
Stir Up Some Happiness   121
The Warning Spell   119
White Light Protection Spell   119
Witch Bottle of Protection   125

Guide to Practices, Spells, and Recipes   229

Beltane Recipes
Bannocks   126
Sorcerous Lentil Salad   128
Spellbound Sugar Cookies   128
Super Moon Refreshment   127

Litha

Practices and Tips
Creating a Personal Pentagram of Intent   133
Working with Wishing Stones   132

Litha Spells
Antianxiety Affirmation   142
Bottle Spell to Get a Raise   140
Bright Summer Solstice/Litha   136
Bug Potion #9   138
Calming Your Pet on the Fourth of July   142
Emotional-Healing Spell   139
Fourth of July Sparkling Wish Spell   141
The Healing Bubble   145
Leadership Quartz Crystal Spell   140
A Midsummer's Dream Spell   144
Release the Anger   145
A Seasoned Witch's Traveling Bag for Meandering Enchantments
   by Sam Miller   147
Summer Magick Spell Jar   137
To Tell the Truth Spell   143

Litha Recipes
A Blink of the Eye Hawaiian Pie   155

230   *Magick for All Seasons*

Conjured Shredded Chicken in Chili Verde   154

Summer Fruit Salad   153

Lughnasadh/Lammas

Practices and Tips

Crafting a Rustic Magick Wand   158

Creating a Manifestation Box   162

Lughnasadh/Lammas Spells

Burning Bowl Ritual   164

Cat Blessing   170

Clearing Your Head Invocation   171

Floating in Air Morning Affirmation   172

Flush Your Troubles Away   173

Magickal Harvest Jar   164

Meditation to Unclutter Your Mind   172

Money Grows Prosperity Spell   169

The Money Tree   168

Simple Money Spell   166

Two Sweet-Smelling Ways to Attract Money   167

Wealth Witch Bottle   166

Yes or No Orange Spell   168

Lughnasadh/Lammas

Charmed Pickled Green Tomatoes   175

Corn Pone   174

Mystical Rice Pudding   174

Guide to Practices, Spells, and Recipes

Mabon

Practices and Tips
Create and Work with an Energy Ball   180
Eye of Newt and Toe of Frog?   178

Mabon Spells
Autumn Leaves Wishes   184
Calm Down!   189
Cinnamon Abundance Spell   183
End Bad Luck   191
House Entry Protection Spell   187
Join Incenses to Boost Your Spells   190
Justice Candle Spell   189
Keeping the House Spirits Happy   185
The Magickal Apple   182
A Nutty Prosperity Spell   183
Return the Favor   192
Salt Protection   186
Spill the Beans   186
To Keep a Spell from Backfiring   191
To Protect Animals from Abuse   188

Mabon Recipes
Conjuring Up a Honey Cake   194
Heartwarming Baked Apples   193
Magickal Black Beans   194
Magickally Marvelous Marinated Mushrooms   193
Saint Jan's Bewitching Banana Nut Tea Bread   195

Memories and the Wheel of the Year—An Exercise   196

ABOUT THE AUTHOR

Marla Brooks is the creator of *The Witch's Oracle* deck and has been the host of *Stirring the Cauldron* on the Para X Radio Network for over fourteen years. She grew up knowing that there was more to this world than the naked eye could see and found the notion of ghosts and other things that go bump in the night rather fascinating. Of course, you might expect that from a witch. Marla didn't just decide one day that she wanted to be a witch—it's just part of who she is. Her great-grandmother Sophie was a witch, and these things often get passed down in the bloodline from generation to generation.

Before publicly coming out of the "broom closet," she worked as a freelance entertainment writer for various national publications, mainly doing celebrity interviews. She is the author of several books in both the metaphysical and mainstream genres, including the Ghosts of Hollywood series, *Workplace Spells*, and *Animal Spells and Magick*; two fiction books, *A Bad Case of the Collywobbles* and *Soul Connection: A Deadly Obsession*; as well as two cookbooks. She lives in Southern California.

TO OUR READERS

Weiser Books, an imprint of Red Wheel/Weiser, publishes books across the entire spectrum of occult, esoteric, speculative, and New Age subjects. Our mission is to publish quality books that will make a difference in people's lives without advocating any one particular path or field of study. We value the integrity, originality, and depth of knowledge of our authors.

Our readers are our most important resource, and we appreciate your input, suggestions, and ideas about what you would like to see published.

Visit our website at *www.redwheelweiser.com*, where you can learn about our upcoming books and free downloads, and also find links to sign up for our newsletter and exclusive offers.

You can also contact us at *info@rwwbooks.com* or at

Red Wheel/Weiser, LLC
65 Parker Street, Suite 7
Newburyport, MA 01950